TRACING YOUR
SECRET
SERVICE
ANCESTORS

An autographed MI5 New Year's card for 1918. The signatures are those of female staff, mostly from A and H Branches.
(with grateful thanks to Dr Nicholas Hiley)

TRACING YOUR
SECRET
SERVICE
ANCESTORS

PHIL TOMASELLI

Pen & Sword
FAMILY HISTORY

ISBN 978 1 84415 987 1

The right of Phil Tomaselli to be identified as Author of the Work
has been asserted by him in accordance with the Copyright,
Designs and Patents Act 1988.

A CIP catalogue record for this book is
available from the British Library.

Typeset in Palatino and Optima by
S L Menzies-Earl

Printed and bound in England by
CPI UK

Pen & Sword Books Ltd incorporates the imprints of
Pen & Sword Aviation, Pen & Sword Maritime, Pen & Sword Military,
Wharncliffe Local History, Pen & Sword Select, Pen & Sword Military Classics
and Leo Cooper

For a complete list of Pen & Sword titles please contact
PEN & SWORD BOOKS LTD
47 Church Street, Barnsley, South Yorkshire, S70 2AS, England
E-mail: enquiries@pen-and-sword.co.uk
Website: www.pen-and-sword.co.uk

CONTENTS

INTRODUCTION

Ten years ago this book was scarcely possible. MI5 records were just beginning to be released; SOE personnel files were not released until 2003. SIS (more popularly MI6) records have not, and probably never will be, released. Even now there are gaps in the material but the diligent researcher stands a reasonable chance of finding out something about the life of an ancestor who worked in one of the secret services between the late Victorian period and the end of the Second World War.

MI5 and SIS are publishing official histories in 2009 and 2010, and an unofficial history of SIS is being written. Hopefully this volume will supplement these publications for people interested in carrying out their own detailed researches into individuals or operations. Where anything differs from the accepted (or even official) histories, I am happy to provide references, if not already quoted, to any researcher who enquires.

I have quoted many useful references and methods for finding others. I have also given details of some of the officers, agents and other staff I have researched over the years. There is no guarantee, however, that other investigations will produce the same kind of results. One diligent researcher, following an alleged British agent in Russia during the First World War, has checked every source and followed up every lead and still cannot confirm his tale. Many records were destroyed at the time or are likely to be retained indefinitely. But it is always worth trying.

This is a résumé of research I have carried out over the course of twenty years, mainly at The National Archives (TNA) but also at other archives. I began looking at intelligence records while researching the Intervention War in Russia and realised that, contrary to expectation, some secret-service material was available in records belonging to various government departments. An interest developed in the intelligence community generally and a gradual picture has emerged of the various organisations and how they interacted. Releases in the last ten years have provided much more information.

This book reflects my own interests and prejudices – I have not touched British involvement in Ireland, nor the intelligence work done by the Special Forces during the Second World War. I have included some of the more esoteric organisations such as the Auxiliary Units (the British Resistance) and the British Army Aid Group (BAAG), which ran supplies into prisoner-of-war camps in Hong Kong, and did a little spying along the way.

Everyone who worked for the intelligence services signed the Official Secrets Act and will have had it explained to them, **in no uncertain terms**, the consequences of breaking it. Even though there may be records released from their service (MI5 or SOE), they may not feel their personal obligations to maintain secrecy have been discharged. Even after their deaths the administrators of their estates are likely to receive letters stressing that any material they had in their possession was the property of the Government and should be returned. Please, as much for your own sake as theirs, do not put living relatives under undue pressure to tell you what they might have done.

One important thing I would ask any reader who investigates a relative and finds out anything about their secret work is that they write it up and make it publicly available. The official histories are likely to be thin on personal detail apart perhaps from a few people at the very top, but it is the people who do the actual work, who look up the records, carry the messages, break the cyphers, follow the suspects, analyse the information and, on occasion, blow up the target or steal the information, upon which everything depends. Every scrap of information you find could be invaluable in building up a detailed history of the whole.

I would like to stress that all the information included about individuals has been derived from publicly accessible documents, some of which have been open for many years.

ACKNOWLEDGEMENTS

I owe a great debt to many people who have helped me, provided information and advice, as well as documents and photographs. My friends Professor Rick Spence of Idaho University and Dr Nicholas Hiley of the University of Kent have both greatly assisted me in understanding their particular specialities, and Nick kindly provided some of the illustrations. David List has long been an inspiration and mentor in my investigations, explaining patiently the importance of understanding exactly what individual documents mean, how they relate to one another and acting as a sounding board on later SOE and SIS operations. Julian Putkowski has been a fount of interesting information on obscure sources and themes, as well as providing many good laughs and illustrations from the MI5 cartoon book. Bryan Clough shared a great deal of information on Maxwell Knight, Fascism and the Harker brothers. Peter and Wenche Georgiadis deserve many thanks for allowing me to use Peter's grandfather as an illustration of what can be found out about an individual if you are lucky and diligent. Major Ian Tomes and the Tomes Family History Society were invaluable in finding background on Sidney Tomes. Griselda Brooks kindly shared with me her researches into her uncle John Darwin. Dr Simon Leather provided me with information and photographs on John Leather. Dr John Salt translated French newspaper reports on the Leather case. Jan Keoghan at RNAS Yeovilton helped track down Lieutenant O'Caffrey and gave me access to the RNVR officers' ledgers. The staffs of Swindon libraries found many obscure books and articles for me. Michael Smith, author of some excellent books on the subject, provided help and clarification on several matters. The staff of The National Archives have always been kind, helpful and professional and helped me find obscure documents. John Warwicker kindly showed me round the British Resistance Museum and provided information on the organisation and its members. I owe grateful thanks to Rena for the Collas papers and permission to use his photograph, and to Linda Pascal for putting us in contact. John Gallehawke kindly showed me round the Bletchley Park archives. Simon Fowler has acted as my friend and editor over several years.

My dear wife, Francine, has had to put up with my researches since before we were married and has always been supportive and encouraging and has listened patiently while I explained my latest discoveries and theories. I owe her a very great debt for her support and tolerance and dedicate this book to her.

Chapter 1

GETTING STARTED

Experienced family historians will already be aware that the more you know about an ancestor at the start of your quest, the more you are likely to find out as you go on. Though the documents that you will be looking for (or at) in the case of secret-service people are likely to be different from the usual family history documents, the principle is the same. Collect together all the information you can find and write it down.

Gathering information
Look out any paperwork you might have; speak to your relatives, particularly the older ones, to see if they have any relevant medals, diaries, official papers, passports, letters or memorabilia that might be useful to you. Ask if they remember any stories they might have been told about where your relative served and what they did – though such stories need to be treated with a certain amount of caution, there is often a germ of truth in them. Ask if your relative had any particular language skills, if they know whether they went abroad – and if they did, find out approximately when and where they went. Try and find out the names of people they worked with as sometimes their friends and contacts can provide a vital clue.

Please remember that someone who has been engaged in secret work will have been warned that they should not discuss their work. This may well have extended to warning their relatives not to talk about anything and many people will want to respect this wish.

Family historians will know that very often you will find out more information about someone when something goes wrong in their life – divorce, bankruptcy, serious injury, a trial or conviction, scandal and death – these types of thing generate publicity and paperwork. The quiet, law-abiding citizen is harder to find information on. So it is in the world of secret service – the good spy, whether an administrator at headquarters, officer in the field or agent operating under cover should generate as little paperwork as possible. You tend to get more information when something goes wrong and other people become involved. The cases of John Leather and George Georgiadis, who were both imprisoned, are good examples. Most of the time you are likely only to find brief definite confirmation of involvement with secret service and will then have to make generalisations about their work by reading associated documents.

Useful things to have at the start

- Full name and date of birth of the person you are researching;
- Write down why you think why they might have been involved in secret-service work;
- Name(s) of likely next of kin (father, mother or spouse);
- Collect any photographs, letters, postcards, pieces of uniform or other kit that come from their period of service.

Some of this information you'll need in order to obtain a copy of the individual's service record or to check that you have found the correct service record if it has already been released to the public.

In the period we are looking at there is a very strong chance that your relative served in one of the armed forces either as a 'cover' for their real work, because they started in the forces and transferred, or simply as an administrative means of getting them paid. Find out which of the services they served in – the Army, Royal Navy (including Royal Marines) or Royal Air Force – and try and work out the dates they served. Details of the regiment and battalion, ship or squadron will also speed up your search. Try and find out whether they were an officer or 'other rank'. Though the better known secret-service people were generally officers, many 'other ranks' did administrative and technical work.

Armed forces personal service records

Everyone who serves in the armed forces has a unique service record, which gives basic details of what they did, where they went, their promotions, medals and next of kin. The first thing to decide is whether their record might be available at TNA, or whether you will need to apply to the Ministry of Defence for a copy.

The Royal Navy

Royal Navy officer service records for those who joined the service before May 1917 are in ADM 196. These are now available online and on microfilm at TNA and the records have been indexed and the results are on cards held in the Open Reading Room. They contain such information as dates of birth, rank, seniority, date of appointment, orders and commissions, awards, distinctions and examinations and include particulars of Royal Marine officers. There are record cards additionally for all naval officers born before 1900 in ADM 340. There is a useful TNA leaflet on finding RN officers' service records available online at: http://www.nationalarchives.gov.uk/catalogue/RdLeaflet.asp?sLeafletID=261.

Service records of RNVR officers can be found in two series: ADM 337. The records in ADM 337/117 – ADM 337/128 cover the period up to 1922 and are searchable by name on TNA's online catalogue: http://www.nationalarchives.gov.uk/catalogue/Default.asp?j=l.

The best place to find records for Royal Naval Reserve officers is in ADM 340 – Richard Tinsley, SIS man in Holland in the First World War, is in ADM 340/136 and Basil Ohlson, an early MI5 officer, is in ADM 340/104.

Service records for Royal Naval ratings who joined the Royal Navy between 1873 and 1923 are in the ADM 188 series. These records can now be accessed at TNA's online catalogue. These records do not give service details after 1928.

There is a useful TNA leaflet on finding RN ratings' service records available online at: http://www.nationalarchives.gov.uk/catalogue/RdLeaflet.asp?sLeafletID=39#3.

If the service record is not yet open, you can apply (if you are next of kin or can obtain their consent) to have a copy by contacting: The Directorate of Personnel Support (Navy), Navy Search, TNT Archive Services, Tetron Point, William Nadin Way, Swadlincote, Derbyshire DE11 0BB; tel: 01283 227 910/911/912/913; fax: 01283 227 942; email: navysearchpgrc@tnt.co.uk.

For Royal Marine officers from 1893 to 1925 there are detailed service records in ADM 196/58-65, 83 and 97-112.

Records for Royal Marine other ranks are in ADM 157 (Attestation Forms) and ADM 159 (Service Records) and there is a TNA guide available online at: http://www.nationalarchives.gov.uk/catalogue/RdLeaflet.asp?sLeafletID=56.

For records of both officers and other ranks after 1923 you will need to apply to: The Directorate of Personnel Support (Navy), Navy Search, TNT Archive Services, Tetron Point, William Nadin Way, Swadlincote,

Derbyshire DE11 0BB; tel: 01283 227 910/911/912/913; fax: 01283 227 942; email: navysearchpgre@tnt.co.uk.

The Army

Service records for Army officers who served before 1913 and did not serve during the First World War are in WO 25 and WO 76. A useful TNA guide is available online at: http://www.nationalarchives.gov.uk/catalogue/RdLeaflet.asp?sLeafletID=13.

Service records for officers who served in the First World War and up to about 1922 are in WO 339 and WO 374 series. We will look at the contents in more depth later, but to begin with it is necessary to find the record. If the surname is reasonably unusual then a search can be made using TNA's online catalogue in the two series, otherwise you will need to visit TNA and use the microfilmed index in WO 338, which is an alphabetical list of officers that will give you (by a circuitous route) the reference you will require.

Service records for Army other ranks from the First World War were badly damaged in the blitz and only some 2 million survive, in one form or another, out of about 9 million originals. The surviving records are in WO 363 and WO 364. These records are going online at ancestry.com.

A useful TNA guide is available online at: http://www.nationalarchives.gov.uk/catalogue/RdLeaflet.asp?sLeafletID=18#8.

If you are searching for someone who served after 31 March 1922 the records are still with the Ministry of Defence. You can apply (if you are next of kin or can obtain their consent) to have a copy by contacting: Ministry of Defence, Army Personnel Centre, Historic Disclosures, Mailpoint 400, Kentigern House, 65 Brown Street, Glasgow G2 8EX; tel: 01412 242 023/3 303; email: disc4.civsec@apc.army.mod.uk.

The Home Guard

Though promised for some time, Home Guard records have not yet been released. The Home Guard List gives details of officers and is available on the shelves of TNA's Open Reading Room.

Next of kin can apply to: Army Personnel Centre, Historic Disclosures, Mailpoint 555, Kentigern House, 65 Brown Street, Glasgow G2 8EX; tel: 08456 009 663.

Royal Air Force

The Royal Air Force (RAF) was formed on 1 April 1918 by amalgamating the Army's Royal Flying Corps (RFC) and the Royal Naval Air Service (RNAS). Officers and men of both services transferred into the new service and were joined by new entrants.

Records of RFC officers, 1914–March 1918, were forwarded to the RAF and are in AIR 76, along with records of RAF officers who joined after April 1918 and details of former RNAS officers after that date. Records of RNAS officers up to March 1918, are in ADM 273.

Service Records for both officers who served after 1922 and men who served after 1924 are still retained by the Ministry of Defence and to access these you will need to write to: RAF Disclosures Section, Room 221b, Trenchard Hall, RAF Cranwell, Sleaford, Lincolnshire NG34 8HB; tel: 01400 261 201 ext 6711, exts 8161/8159 (officers), exts 8163/8168/8170 (other ranks).

When writing to any of the service-record offices, please provide not only proof of kinship but as much information as you can regarding your relative, including full name, date and place of birth and a rough idea of his period of service. Most important of all, if you have his service number, give that first – service numbers in the RAF have always been unique. A fee is chargeable.

Other things you can do

There are some very good histories of the various secret services that your local library may have, or that they may be able to obtain for you through the inter-library loan service. I have included these in the bibliography.

Useful things to know

The National Archives

This may seem like an advertisement for The National Archives at Kew (TNA) because almost all the official papers you are going to want are held there. There are other sources that may be able to provide additional information in the form of personal papers of people who may have served with them but in the main it is TNA that will be the source of the information you will want to access.

If you have Internet access start by looking at TNA website at: http://www.nationalarchives.gov.uk/default.htm. The first page includes links to some guides to starting family history research and there is a basic introducion to some of the intelligence records they hold (including MI5 and Special Operations Executive) online at: http://www.nationalarchives. gov.uk/catalogue/RdLeaflet.asp?sLeafletID=32.

Try, quite simply, entering the individual's name into TNA's search engine and see what pops up. Obviously with a name like Smith you are going to get a lot of hits (917 alone in WO 374) but persevere, restrict the date range and series searched and try adding initials etc. When I first started doing this research very few records could be searched for in this way, but now the initial searching is so much easier. George Georgiadis pops up in FO 286/730 and HO 144/6272 immediately.

Take time to look at TNA's website in advance of any visit you intend making. The 'Visit Us' page will give information on how to get there, opening times, document ordering and an initial tour for new visitors. It is well worthwhile taking this tour as it will show you the reading rooms, where to find readers' guides and computer terminals and who to ask for advice.

Photocopying facilities are available, and digital cameras are allowed. Some of the documents you may be interested in (such as First World War medal cards and some of the more popular MI5 records) are available online to download from home but can also be printed off during your visit at considerably reduced cost.

Records at TNA are held under the reference of the Government Department that created them. For the Security Service (MI5) records are in the KV series; for SOE the HS series; for the Government Code & Cypher School (now GCHQ and commonly known as Bletchley Park) the HW series. Other series that may well come into a search are MEPO (Metropolitan Police, for Special Branch); the Home Office (HO series) for records on subversives, internees and naturalised foreigners; the Admiralty (ADM series) for Royal Naval records; the War Office (WO series) for the Army and AIR series for the RAF.

Some of the records are so popular that they are held on microfilm, including officer and other rank RAF service records from the First World War in AIR 76 and AIR 79, soldiers' service records in WO 363 and WO 364 and MI5's First World War records in KV 1. Microfilm readers and copiers are available, and you can request to see the original documents in special cases.

With the best will in the world, unless you are very lucky and only looking for a small amount of information, you are unlikely to find everything you want on your first visit. Set your sights reasonably low – if you already have a service record that shows where the individual served, try finding a few files relating to their postings to begin with.

Don't be afraid to ask the staff if you do not understand something – I have always found them very friendly and professional, and their range of knowledge of the records is incredible.

Freedom of Information Act

The Freedom of Information Act does not apply to SIS, MI5, Special Branch or GCHQ, but this does not mean that it cannot be used to find information that may be relevant to research.

On occasion you may come across a file that is at TNA but that is marked 'Closed or Retained Document' but which you think may be of interest to you. If this is the case, the catalogue itself should offer you the opportunity to request a review. Many of the Home Office naturalisation papers and most of the SOE personnel files are like this if the individual's date of birth is less than 100 years ago. You will need to provide evidence that the individual is dead. For policy files marked 'Closed or Retained Document' there is no need to provide a reason, and you will be advised of the decision in due course.

Some files are 'Closed Or Retained Document, Open Description, Retained by Department under Section 3.4'. For these you will need to apply to the relevant department for a review.

Overlap

It is worth bearing in mind that there has always been a considerable exchange of staff (and sometimes even agents) between the various intelligence organisations. MI5 has taken Special Branch officers from time to time, MI5 officers have gone to work for SIS on a regular basis and vice versa, SOE and SIS exchanged staff and the Auxiliary Units provided officers and men for Special Forces and SOE. The Intelligence Corps has served as a source of officers and agents and as a convenient badge for agents to wear in the field to try and protect them from charges of being a spy.

If you are unable to trace a relative in the records of the service you thought they were in, then it is worth digging around a bit more. For example, John Patrick Shelley was in MI5 in the First World War and his subsequent career (too long to go into here) encompassed Military Intelligence, SIS, Passport Control, SOE and Special Forces in the Far East. His career has had to be reconstructed from records relating to all of these services.

Ancestral sources frequently work just as well on spies

Just because you are looking at someone involved in secret-service work it does not mean that other family history resources will not apply. Censuses available online can be used to find dates of birth and family connections and there are various passenger lists and immigration lists online, as well as online newspapers such as *The Times*, which frequently refer to individuals.

One minor problem that I was able to solve with the help of online documents was the exact identity of the man who took over as Director of MI5 in May 1940. The introduction to the first MI5 official history names him as Brigadier A W A Harker, as does (in May 2008) the official MI5 website. (This has subsequently been amended to O A Harker – however they are still wrong in saying he was from the Army; he was a former Indian policeman.) The Organisational Structure Charts in the official history, as well as staff lists in KV 4/127, say it should be Brigadier O A Harker. Another slight mystery concerning O A Harker was quite where he came from – he suddenly emerges on the MI5 staff lists in quite a senior position – he must have had previous intelligence connections, but what were they?

The Times Digital Archive (TDA) was my primary source. This provides a digitised source of *The Times* newspaper from 1785–1875. Some local libraries will allow you access from your home computer and other libraries (and TNA) will allow you access from theirs.

Among the facts obtained were:
• An announcement on 5 June 1919 of the forthcoming marriage of Major A W Allen Harker RGA;

Seen here in his uniform as an officer in the Grenadier Guards, J P Shelley served successively in the King's Own Royal Lancaster Regiment, MI5, the Royal Flying Corps, on attachment to the Egyptian Army, Military Intelligence in China, with SIS in the Middle East, as Passport Control Officer in Warsaw, with SOE in the Middle East and with Special Forces in India. (courtesy of the Regimental Museum of the King's Own Royal Lancaster Regiment)

• An announcement on 9 August 1919 of Major Harker's marriage on the 7 August. On this occasion his full name (Arthur William Allen Harker) was given;
• An announcement on 29 June 1920 of Oswald Allen Harker's forthcoming marriage;
• An announcement on 27 October 1920 of the marriage of Mr Oswald Allen Harker (Indian Police) the previous day. Captain A W Allen Harker, the bridegroom's brother, was best man. Colonel Sir Vernon and Lady Kell were among the guests;
• An announcement on 5 March 1938 of changes at the War Office that included Lieutenant Colonel A W A Harker, RAOC, as Assistant Director of Munitions Production;
• An announcement on 26 October 1945 of Oswald Allen Harper's silver wedding.

Kell's presence at Oswald Harker's wedding and the fact that he had been in the Indian Police confirm that he was the MI5 man and explained his previous intelligence connection. The Indian Civil Service List at TNA was able to give me more information about his previous career.

The only Oswald Harker in the 1901 Census was an agricultural worker living in Yorkshire, which sounded unlikely. The 1891 Census produced a more likely prospect, Oswald Allan Harker, aged 5, born in Cirencester, Gloucestershire. His brother Arthur is shown as being born in 1890. Their father was Professor James Allen Harker, naturalist on the faculty at the Royal Agricultural College, Cirencester; their mother was a playwright and novelist writing as Lizzie Allen Harker (her married name) or just Lizzie Allen.

Armed with this information, it was easy to find the Harkers in the 1891 Census but not in the 1901 Census for some reason. In 1891, Oswald's age was given as 5 and Arthur's as 6 months. Records of their births in 1886 and 1890 were then easily obtained using Findmypast.com.

Findmypast.com was also then used to find Oswald's death. This was a laborious search, quarter by quarter, until his name appeared in the January–March Quarter 1968. He had died in Lambeth at the age of 81.

From the Army lists, I was able to establish that although they both finished up as brigadiers, Oswald's was a courtesy title bestowed by the War Office, while Arthur had been a career officer.

The temporary Director of MI5 was Oswald Allen Harker, not his brother as some think.

Useful tools for identifying individuals

Passport records

Before the First World War passports were more or less optional for travel abroad, but immediate restrictions on travel were introduced in 1914, becoming increasingly Draconian as the war progressed. Records of passports issued in Britain are in the form of ledgers, written daily, in the FO 610 series between FO 610/123 and FO 610/137. People travelling on official business were usually given 'gratis passports' issued in the name of the department they were working for, so you will see 'Gratis – War Office' or 'Gratis – Admiralty' in the ledgers. From early 1918 onwards there are details of destinations, but prior to this just a note of the applicant's name, passport number and whether issued gratis. Military and Naval officers travelling abroad to neutral and Allied countries, who were not going to the front but were working in missions etc., were usually issued gratis passports, but so were a small number of civilians – a case in point being Sidney Reilly (nicknamed the 'Ace of Spies' and the subject of several biographies) who travelled to Russia in early 1918 and whose passport, dated 24 March 1918, was issued gratis but with no further explanation.

Without knowing the date an ancestor might have travelled abroad these records can be long and tedious to trawl, but the gratis usually stands out, saving time in the search.

The Foreign Office card index

Foreign Office papers contain much correspondence relating to SIS, its officers and agents, and there are occasional MI5e papers, so it is useful for researchers to have a grasp of the way that the papers were originally referenced and how they are now collected.

Correspondence comprised telegrams and letters from embassies and consulates worldwide, as well as from individuals, companies and other interested parties, and the Foreign Office's replies. Each piece of correspondence was numbered and sent to the relevant section which would act on it and decide which file it would be stored in. The numbering sequence started afresh every year.

In 1906 the Foreign Office adopted a card index which allowed the same piece of correspondence to be indexed under several different headings, and the various headings to be kept together for each calendar year. A person who travelled regularly and came to the Foreign Office's attention in more than one country should have one or more cards, headed with their

Christian Names (in full)		*Sidney*			Permanent Home} Address		*George.*	
Date of Birth								

Name of Person to be } Informed of Casualties }   Name   *Mrs. a. Reilly*   Address { *120 Broadway.* *USA*

Date Sheet Started   9. 8. 18 | Registered Pa|

MOVEMENTS

Outgoing Authority	Unit from which	Unit to which	Date of Effect	Special Remarks re Duties	Incoming Authority Confirming	Outgoing Authority	U:
		Canada	3.12.14	Appt 2bs.			
671096 8.19.18		War office State he was employed by them in conjunction with Foreign office on special missions from March 1918 to date of Demob					
		Employed by war office (MI.I.C) from March 1918 to December 1918					
		Employed on Special Mission by Foreign office December 1918 to April 1919.					
		Employed by war office (MI.IC) from April 1919 to date of demob.					
		Protection certificate states, Russia					
Nov. 19.		eligible for gratuity					
16. 12. 25 The Aeroplane		Killed 28.9.25 near the Village of ALLEKUL, Russia, by O.G.P.U. troops.					

APPOI

Date of Lond. Gaz.	R
28/1/18 (1418)	T 1
28/1/18 (1419)	T 2
A.F.L.	2.
4.5.20 5106.	½

Made famous by the book and television series Ace of Spies, *Sidney Reilly's RAF service record clearly shows his work for MI1c, a First World War cover name for SIS. (via the Fleet Air Arm Museum, Yeovilton)* name with a brief summary of each reference and a series of numbers pointing to the file location of the individual correspondence.

The actual correspondence is held in various Foreign Office series of records at TNA in the form of bound volumes. The card index, key to finding individual documents, is in the Document Reading Room.

Before the First World War there were five basic categories of correspondence and each is now kept in a separate series. Political correspondence is in FO 371 series; commercial correspondence is in FO 368; consular in FO 369; treaty in FO 372; and African colonies prior to 1913 in FO 367. New departments were created during the war in response to specific problems. The blockade of Germany resulted in the creation of the Contraband Department, the papers for which are in FO 382 (including coal and shipping papers); prisoners-of-war correspondence is in FO 383; and a News Department, which monitored the foreign press for pro-German stories and distributed British propaganda, correspondence for which is in FO 395.

Within each series the correspondence was filed by country, and each country was assigned a unique number that applied across all the series. Russia was always 38, Germany was always 13 and Switzerland 43. In addition to this number each department had their own number: political correspondence simply began with the country number but consular correspondence added a 2 at the beginning (so that 238 is consular/Russia), treaty is prefaced with a 3, African colonies prefaced with a 4, contraband with 11, prisoners of war with 12, news with N and coal and shipping with 21.

Each piece of correspondence had its own unique number for the year it came in and was either assigned to an already existing file or became the start of a new file if it was on a new subject. If a new piece came in on, for example, the political reporting of Arthur Ransome, a British journalist in Russia in 1917, it would be numbered (say 456987) and if a new file was considered necessary it would be given the same number and indexed as: 38 f 456987 or 38 456987. Files were referenced by either a prefix f or by underlining the number. If the file was related to the Consular Department the reference would be: 238 456987 or 238 f 456987 and if related to the News Department the reference would be N38 456987 or N38 f 456987.

If a subsequent piece came in, with its own unique number of 462113 and it was felt it related to the same subject then it would be filed with it and referenced 38 462113/456987. The second number is the file number and the first is the paper number. The index card (held in this case in the cards for

1917) would include a very brief résumé of each piece and, when the card was full, a second one would be started and filed behind the first.

Once you have noted this reference you will need to find TNA indexes for the series in which the papers are held. Assuming that the file you are interested in is Political, find the bound index for FO 371 covering 1917 (the staff will point these out to you) and look for the section covering Russia. Find the file number and check, if the Foreign Office file is spread across more than one TNA file, the range of papers and select the one covering the paper(s) you are interested in. Having ordered the TNA file you then go through it until you locate the individual Foreign Office file and the paper within it.

Some files were, by virtue of their subject, very large indeed, and span up to a dozen TNA files. I have been working through the files for eighteen years and they still occasionally throw up a reference that surprises me. NC 38, for example, refers to a sub-section of the News (FO 395) files on Russia dealing with news censorship. If in doubt, ask the staff, who are very helpful and knowledgeable.

Searching the indexes

It can take a while to get used to the index cards and to the bureaucratic mindset that created and used them. When looking for an individual the obvious place to start is with any cards made out in their name, which should produce references to any correspondence specific to them, or to correspondence in which their name is mentioned. The latter approach is not infallible so it is possible the person you are interested in might be referred to in correspondence that is only indexed under a more general heading. If they were working as a journalist in Russia, try looking for cards headed 'journalists', 'press correspondents', the name of their newspaper or even, in extremity, 'Russia' (and look through the numerous cards under that heading for anything that might apply). If you know a particular place, you can try looking for cards with references under that heading, e g., 'St Petersburg' or 'Moscow'. If you do identify a file that contains information you are looking for, it is worth checking the whole file, not just the papers listed in the card index, as sometimes material slipped through the indexer's net. Sometimes the only way to find material is to read carefully through dozens of files – if nothing else the material is usually fascinating, if not strictly relevant to what you are looking for.

There is a good basic guide to the card index available online at: http://www.nationalarchives.gov.uk/catalogue/RdLeaflet.asp?sLeafletID=280.

Foreign Office indexes after 1919

Card indexes continued after 1919 but are retained by the Foreign Office Archive in Milton Keynes. Instead, there are index books from 1920 to 1951 on the open shelves in TNA's search room. They are alphabetical by subject, so that individuals appear exactly where you would expect them, but subjects such as conferences tend to be grouped together and international relations between countries are indexed under the first country alphabetically, e.g., French/Russian relations are all indexed under France, whereas Russian/Swiss relations are all indexed under Russia. There is a clear indication as to how SIS was organised as under 'Secret Service, British' you are referred to 'Passport Control'.

There was a gradual increase in the number of Foreign Office departments so the references can be a little more complex than the card indexes, but at the front of almost every index volume you will find lists of country and departmental references you can use to locate the files and documents that you are interested in.

Foreign Office green indexes

The 'green' series of secret papers were indexed separately from the normal ones and contain references for the more sensitive papers. These are bound together with the ordinary pieces and are distinguishable by their file covers having a green band across the top.

Green paper indexes 1920 to 1938 are bound into one volume, while 1939 and 1940 have their own green indexes but after this indexes have been released. It is interesting to speculate that perhaps the SIS 'red' and Code & Cypher School 'blue' files had their own indexes, but if so these have not been released.

After 1924 the FO weeded their records more regularly than previously so that some records are not on the file. Some of these may have been SIS reports but many seem to have been destroyed as being of no interest. The card index in Milton Keynes will frequently contain a little bit more information than the bound index and copies can be requested by contacting: Information Rights Team, Information Management Group, Foreign and Commonwealth Office, Old Admiralty Building, London SW1A 2PA; tel: 02070 080 123; email: dp-foi.img@fco.gov.uk. Your request must be in writing, which includes emails as well as letters, and should include:

- details of the information you would like to see (please be as precise as you can); and
- your name and postal address.

Home Office naturalisation papers

A number of SIS and MI5 officers and agents have found themselves in a confused legal position regarding their status as British (or other) citizens and these situations have had to be resolved through the Home Office naturalisation process. Their papers are at TNA along with the thousands of others who have been naturalised over the years. The 'background papers' accompanying each application can be most instructive, see especially the naturalisation papers for Pierre Marie Cavrois O'Caffrey (HO 144/3470). Several other released documents shed interesting light on the backgrounds of the people who served this country secretly.

Among the earliest was Henry (Harry) Lambton Carr, Assistant Passport Control Officer then Passport Control Officer, Helsinki (1920 to 1940.) His papers are in HO 144/11056. Carr's nationality was questioned when his cousin, Robert Carr, applied for naturalisation citing Henry's PCO status and his having a British passport in his support. Related papers in FO 372/2500 explain how their great-grandfather, Matthew Carr, born in Northumberland, had founded the Baltic Ironworks at St Petersburg. The file includes two letters from Admiral Sinclair (his signature has been removed by cutting away the lower part of the page but his references C/3481 and C/3529 are still visible). Home Office investigations revealed that both Carr's father and paternal grandfather had been in born in Russia. Carr was therefore 'an alien of no nationality', even though he had held British passports since 1910. Sinclair was keen to have the position resolved and suggested Carr be granted naturalisation in the form of a 'Special Certificate in case of doubt'. Home Office officials granted naturalisation on the grounds of Carr's services under the Crown, including time in the Army and his service in Helsinki. At the urging of the Helsinki Legation they even found precedent for the usual £10 fee to be waived.

Background application papers from the period between 1844 and 1871 are in TNA series HO 1; between 1872 and 1878 in HO 45; HO 144 covers 1879 to 1934 and HO 405 papers between 1934 and 1948. In this final series only papers for people with initials between A and N have been released to TNA so far. All four series have been indexed on line and can be searched using TNA's website search engine at: http://www.nationalarchives.gov.uk/catalogue.

Chapter 2

EARLY DAYS

Victorian intelligence organisations

Military intelligence

When the British Army sailed for the Crimea in 1854 the only instructions issued to officers on gathering information was an exact reprint of instructions issued during the Napoleonic War. Maps were virtually non-existent. Fortunately a set of plans for the defences of Sebastopol were found by a retired Indian Army officer, Thomas Jervis, in an obscure Belgian bookshop. A civilian, Charles Cattley, born in St Petersburg and a former vice consul, at Kertch on the Crimea, wangled himself the post of Head of Intelligence and his local knowledge, when actually taken notice of, was invaluable. He ran a network of spies and interrogated prisoners but died of cholera in July 1855. The official history of the war said 'the gathering of knowledge by clandestine means were repulsive to the feelings of the English gentleman'.

Following the war there were reviews of the various departments but it took time for a military intelligence organisation to emerge. Major Jervis had established a Topographical and Statistical Department but this was merged with the Ordnance Survey in 1869 and lost its intelligence function. The stunning success of the Prussian Army in the Franco-Prussian War of 1870 was attributed to accurate intelligence and this prompted further developments in the British system. In 1873 an Intelligence Branch was formed at the War Office under Major General Sir Patrick Mcdougal, and this collected maps and information on foreign armies and issued reports.

The department did not employ spies as such, though its officers did go on fishing and sporting trips to foreign countries and collected information as they travelled. Junior officers were encouraged, with the aid of small grants, to undertake travels into interesting areas and to produce reports on their return. Lord Baden-Powell, founder of the Boy Scout movement, records several such trips in his *The Adventures of a Spy*, including pretending to be drunk to deflect the interest of a policeman while spying on a rifle range and collaborating with a fellow 'spy' to attract a sentry's attention while mapping fortifications. Brigadier General W H-H Waters was another Intelligence Department officer who undertook a mission into Russian Poland in 1891 to look for suspicious troop movements. As in all these missions, 'it was intimated to me quite clearly that, if there should be any trouble with the Russian authorities, the War Office would not only disown me altogether but would likewise inflict punishment in order to show perfectly clean hands' (W H-H Waters, *Secret and Confidential – The Experiences of a Mlitary Attaché*). Waters made a successful tour, travelling openly but by night to avoid staying in hotels and having to fill out reports for the police. He had been working in cooperation with the Germans and on his return to Germany he spent ten hours writing down all the information he had committed to memory during the trip. The German General Staff's chief intelligence officer congratulated him with, 'You know, you have given us the most valuable information'.

Tracing Intelligence Department officers

Tracing officers is always easier than tracing ordinary soldiers. There are two published lists for the period and both are available on the open shelves at TNA. Large regional libraries may have copies of the War Office list or be able to obtain copies of either list through the inter-library loan system for a modest fee.

The official *Army List*, published quarterly by the War Office, will tell you which regiment an officer served in, his rank and any attachments to War Office Departments, including Intelligence. There is an index of officers, which will show you the page(s) he appears on. You can trace his previous promotions and his later career by looking at earlier and later editions. The list also contains a record of retirements, casualties and officers who have ceased to serve for other reasons (such as dismissal, cashiering and transportation for military offences) but, though it gives the name and regiment, it rarely gives any more information.

The privately published *Hart's Army List* contains the same details but also, for most of the Victorian period, is likely to give more information on any active service taken part in. Hart's can save you some work looking back at an officer's career because it lists his various promotions to date.

The War Office list, which is also available on the open shelves at TNA, also includes officers attached to the Intelligence Department. Also part of the intelligence organisation were the military attachés working abroad in the capitals of foreign countries. Though their work was open and above board, many had previously worked in the Intelligence Department section covering the country they were later sent to. Brigadier General W H-H Waters served for five years as an attaché in Russia 1893–1898 and again during the First World War with the Military Mission. Lists of attachés can be found in the *Army List* and, as they were attached to the Foreign Office, in the Foreign Office list.

Intelligence records
Records from the period, mainly written reports rather than 'raw' intelligence material, are usually in the WO 32, WO 33 and WO 106 series, with maps in the WO 78 series. WO 106 continues to have releases made of material that is well over 100 years old: WO 106/6390 – 'Précis of the Ashanti Expedition, 1873–1874: by the Intelligence Department, Horse Guards', from 1874, has only been released recently, as has WO 106/6380 – 'Report on the Nile and country between Dongala, Suakin, Kassala and Omdurman'. One has to suspect that they are released not because of any secret content but because officials at the Ministry of Defence found them when tidying up. As the bulk of intelligence work was done by officers there is a good chance of finding material relating to an individual by diligent digging through the papers.

When searching for material using TNA's online search engine do not restrict yourself to using 'intelligence' as a key word, but experiment with country names and ranges of subject. WO 33/28 – 'Memorandum on probable course of action to be adopted by Russia in the event of her attempting to occupy Bulgaria and march on Constantinople' – is clearly an intelligence appreciation but has to be found by using Russia as a key word.

Naval Intelligence
Collection of intelligence has always been an important part of a naval officer's job but the Admiralty did not have a department coordinating and circulating the material. In 1883 a theoretical paper on intelligence by Captain John Colomb persuaded the Admiralty to establish a Foreign Intelligence Committee (FIC) under Captain William Hall, with one Royal Marine officer and three civilian staff. Second Lieutenant George Aston (Royal Marine Artillery) was posted to the FIC in 1886. Expecting an

exciting career of espionage, he was surprised to be set the task of finding out details of British defences at her ports at home and abroad. No one had previously collated this information. Having found where Hong Kong was from an atlas he sat down and began his work there. He was also told to learn about 'submarine telegraph cables, foreign guns, gun mountings, ammunition, armour, electric lights, torpedoes, submarine mines, and experiments therewith' (George Aston, *Secret Service*). Two other officers had divided the world's navies between them and each studied their group, finding out about ships, coastal defences and ports. At about the time that Aston joined, the FIC became the Naval Intelligence Department (NID).

Occasionally Aston took part in active intelligence collection. He travelled to northern France to investigate rumours that new harbour works were designed for a surprise invasion of England and found himself handicapped by his poor French: 'I remember asking my way to the sea, and being understood to want my mother.' (George Aston, *Secret Service*). On another occasion he produced a report on a huge gun displayed at the Paris Exhibition. After his report was submitted he discovered that the gun had been made of papier mâché. In 1892 he was appointed Intelligence Officer to HMS *Victoria* in the Mediterranean, the first appointment of its kind in the Navy. For three years he paid for his work out of the proceeds of a small legacy he had inherited. He made the post such a success that it was formalised when he left in 1895 and he was replaced by another officer sent out by the Intelligence Department in London.

Most of the information that came in to NID was provided by patriotically motivated Britons connected with the sea. No doubt these included the various shipbuilders, Lloyds Insurance and Admiralty representatives abroad. Gradually the various naval stations abroad began to appoint their own intelligence officers, who collected information in their area and circulated it via London.

Finding NID officers
The Admiralty published the *Navy List* on a quarterly basis. You can trace an officer's promotions by looking through a run of the List and it will tell you when he was promoted to his current rank. The List will also tell you which ship the officer was serving on, or which department of the Admiralty he was posted to. Because there is an index of names it is possible to trace an officer's movements from posting to posting throughout his career.

Naval Intelligence reports

There are many Naval Intelligence reports in ADM 231 series from 1883 onwards but, unfortunately, they are not indexed online. Therefore, these need to be searched individually to locate relevant material, though they are chronological, which helps if you know when your officer was in Naval Intelligence.

The Boer War

The Boer War, 1899–1902, was the biggest conflict that the British Army took part in between Waterloo and the start of the First World War. Over 400,000 British and Commonwealth troops fought a long, hard and dangerous war against the armies of the Orange Free State and Transvaal and, when the two republics surrendered, against guerrilla forces that refused to surrender. It was an enormous test for the British Army and its intelligence-gathering capabilities and analysis of its successes and failures were vitally important for the development of organisations and techniques used in the First World War. Many intelligence officers got their first real experience of the work during this war.

The War Office Intelligence Department had made several assessments of the Boer threat, pointing out that the republics were storing up arms purchased abroad. After the war their projections of Boer strength were seen to be remarkably accurate, but they failed to bring home to their chiefs the extent of the danger. When the Boer commandos struck across in October 1899 the British were unprepared for the scale and nature of the fighting to come.

Sir George White was sent to South Africa to take command and took with him Captain Altham of the Colonial Section of the Intelligence Department to supervise the intelligence organisation. Such was the lack of knowledge in London that reports on Boer positions and events on the battlefield, drawn up by the intelligence section for Queen Victoria, had to be culled from press reports sent home by journalists attached to the British Army.

In January 1900, faced with innumerable setbacks, White was replaced as Commander in Chief by Lord Roberts, who took Colonel G Henderson with him as Director of Intelligence. Henderson, in turn, took Major William Robertson with him as an intelligence officer on the staff.

The Headquarters Intelligence Staff consisted of Henderson and five officers ranked as Deputy Assistant Adjutant Generals (DAAGs) who received, recorded, collated and circulated all information regarding the enemy, prepared and distributed maps and charts, provided despatch riders, interpreters, scouts and guides to individual units, scouted the vicinity of the main Army using both white and black scouts, examined captured documents and prisoners and carried out detective work against Boer spies and malcontents. Other DAAGs were appointed to cavalry and mounted infantry divisions and detached units with the job of employing scouts and spies to seek out information on the Boers. Great use was made of the local inhabitants, both black and white, in obtaining information. Both sides did this and there was a tacit agreement that it was legitimate and the men were not treated as true spies might have been, and shot.

Though the British struggled, at least at first, to get good information, they did use tricks of their own to deceive the enemy. Henderson sent out orders by telegram in plain language then countermanded them in cypher and briefed untrustworthy journalists with 'confidential' information, knowing they would betray his apparent trust and circulate the details, so misleading the Boers.

The only route to the sea for the Boers was the railway line running to Laurenco Marques in Portuguese East Africa. This gave the port a particular importance. Under the terms of a secret treaty the British were allowed to use their consulate for intelligence work and the consul, Captain Fritz H E Crowe, ran agents into Boer territory, as well as watching arms transported on the railway. WO 132/21 contains Crowe's diaries and journals of military intelligence with military reports as well as those on political, economic and propaganda matters. A three-page report covering 1–7 May 1900 includes accounts 'from various reliable sources' about the movement of artillery and troops, a report that President Steyn of the Orange Free State had admitted that thousands of Boers troops had gone home and could not be persuaded to return, details of an apparent Boer plan to destroy Johannesburg if it looked likely to fall to the British and on the ill treatment of prisoners of war. It is clear that British residents inside the republics acted as agents and reported back to Crowe. A Mr Munro ('a reliable man') acted both as a messenger for one Sammy Marks, a wealthy Russian-born businessman with interests in coal and gold mining, distilling and canning, and provided information in his own right.

A Mr Broderick, 'who remained in Johannesburg on instructions from us, in order to communicate information through Laurenco Marques', provided reliable reports on the movements of the Boer governments, on supplies, troop movements, entrenchments, ammunitions supplies and the availability of water. Some other agents were natives briefed to carry out long-range scouting missions deep into enemy territory. Refugees seem to have been closely questioned about conditions in the areas they had come from

Later reports include beautiful hand-drawn maps of Boer positions, reports on the companies using Laurenco Marques harbour, their cargoes and carrying capacities, the state of the railways and bridges, troop movements and Boer artillery. It is clear that the Boers realised that information was being gathered at Laurenco Marques as there are reports that only the most reliable people were being allowed through the Transvaal frontier immediately, everyone else being detained a few days so that their information might be out of date by the time it reached the Imperial authorities.

In addition to intelligence work carried out in South Africa, Section H of the Directorate of Military Intelligence was established in London under Major J E Edmonds. It was responsible for 'cable censorship, surveillance of suspected persons in conjunction with Scotland Yard, Press correspondents, enquiries regarding prisoners of war, complaints made by foreigners, violations of Geneva Convention, issue of permits to land in South Africa' (WO 106/6083 'The History of the Directorate of Military Intelligence 1855–1939). A special Permit Office was later created to deal with the last item.

Even after the Boer surrender very careful watch was kept on gun running to South Africa and on the movements of Boer activists. In his personal memoir in KV 1/8, War Office intelligence agent William Melville records watching Boer agents in London. There is further correspondence relating to the prevention of arms being smuggled into South Africa in the years following the war in HD 3/330, HD 3/331 and HD 3/133. There is a note that Laurenco Marques remained a centre for intelligence gathering – the consul continued to receive an allowance to be paid to the Portuguese Chief of Police for information received on suspicious Boers.

Finding Boer War intelligence officers and agents

Details of the worldwide intelligence organisation created for the Boer War are sparse but there is more information on the organisation in South Africa itself.

WO 100/301 and WO 100/354 contain the medal rolls for the Queen's South Africa Medal and King's South Africa Medal for members of the Field Intelligence Department, giving the names of many of the scouts, guides and spies that they employed. A copy of the Roll is held by the Intelligence Corps Museum (see Appendix 1).

WO 108/356 contains a comprehensive list of Field Intelligence Department (FID) personnel serving in South Africa in 1900. The list is in alphabetical order and gives rank and original unit served in. Claude Dansey, a man whose name crops up frequently throughout this book, appears here as 'Lieut Dansey CEM 2 Lancs Fusiliers'. Many of the men were originally with various scout or irregular cavalry units but some are just listed as 'Scout' or 'Agent'.

Crowe's reports in WO 132/21 frequently name his agents and contacts.

WO 32/7844 contains intelligence reports and correspondence on the developing situation in South Africa in the years leading up to the start of the war.

WO 108/270 contains the confidential report on the Intelligence Department drawn up by the Director of Intelligence and is an eight-page summary of their work at a high level.

HD 3/113 and HD 3/126 contain papers and correspondence relating to arms traffic to South Africa and some details of Secret Service budgets during the war.

Some of the scouts and Field Intelligence men went on to serve in the First World War so their records should be held together with their First World War records. Captain Lockhart Henry Larkins of the Tank Corps service record is in WO 374/40835. He was actually nephew of the first head of SIS and had worked for 'C' in the Aegean in 1916 and 1917 before transferring to the Tanks (with whom he was killed in July 1918). His previous service records show that he had served in the Boer War in several major battles with the South African Light Horse before being commissioned in the Cape Railway Sharpshooters in April 1901 'and as Lieutenant commanded Posts and Stations on line De Aar–Mafeking for intelligence purposes, also patrols. Commanded Armoured Train No 10 on Western Line De Aar–Rhodesia for 12 months, was present at all drives on that line 1901/2. Ran Scouts from train for intelligence purposes and was in charge of armoured trains attached to ordinary trains for safe running'.

Special Branch

Though not a secret service but a branch of the Metropolitan Police, Special Branch was, for over a century, in the forefront of the state's counter-espionage and counter-subversion work and most of its records remain closed. Records from before the Second World War are currently being reviewed for release to TNA. It had close connections to the secret services, particularly MI5, for whom it acted as arresting officers and also, at times, as a great rival.

The first Metropolitan Police plain-clothes detectives were established in 1842 and in 1878 a new Criminal Investigation Department (CID) with 240 men was formed. In 1881 a Fenian (Irish Republican) bombing campaign began with attacks on Salford barracks and London's Mansion House. A Fenian Office was created to keep in touch with Home Office experts and the provincial police. On 15 March 1883 two bombs exploded in central London and, next day, a Special Irish Bureau was established at Scotland Yard. Headed by Chief Superintendent Williamson, with a staff of twelve, this became the basis of Special Branch. Special Branch officers were posted to some of the major ports and to key locations on the continent to watch suspects and, working closely with the Royal Irish Constabulary and a Home Office agent in the USA, Henri le Caron, gradually broke the terrorist organisation. Special Branch did work later assumed by specialist units such as VIP protection, investigation of the drugs trade, the shadowing of suspect foreigners and assisting the military authorities during the Boer War. They also watched advocates of Indian independence for the Indian Government and India Office, reporting to Indian Political Intelligence.

Special Branch also watched foreign 'anarchists', which involved liaison with foreign police and secret services. Russia, in particular, was keen to have information on exiled communists in London. William Melville of Special Branch (and later MI5) worked closely with the Russian Pierre Ratchkowsky, who was based in the Russian Embassy in Paris.

Special branch did much of the leg work for MI5, as well as carrying out the arrests of identified spies. HO 45/10892/357291 contains a list of Special Branch officers in February 1918 who were deserving of special thanks from MI5 in respect of 'the numerous enquiries and reports as to aliens and suspected persons' which they had made on the department's behalf. As well as Assistant Commissioner Basil Thomson, Superintendent Quinn and Chief Inspector McBrien, the report names 10 Inspectors, 3 Detective Inspectors, 33 Sergeants and 53 Constables who served with the Branch and 23 other officers from the Central Office.

Special Branch officers also carried out enquiries into aliens within the Metropolitan District as part of their naturalisation process, so many names of Branch officers, as was well as the brief reports they made into prospective claimants, are in the Home Office naturalisation papers in HO 45 and HO 144. The Special Branch report on George Georgiadis contains not only details of the applicant but explanations as to discrepancies in his application. It is signed by Sergeant Palmer and an illegible superintendent, both of Special Branch.

The Home Office Directorate of Intelligence

In 1919 Basil Thomson was appointed head of a Directorate of Intelligence at the Home Office with a special brief for watching subversion throughout Britain. He retained control of Special Branch, with two secret sections (SS1 and SS2) liaising with SIS and provincial chief constables. Thomson's hysterical reports eventually resulted in his having to retire and his Directorate was broken up. Thomson was later arrested for an act of indecency with a prostitute named Thelma De Lava, claiming that he was framed. There are a few records specific to Thomson: HO 144/1590/380368 covers his appointment in 1919; CO 323/853/158 contains an enquiry about one of Thomson's despatches regarding political agitation among coloured peoples; and MEPO 10/10 contains some papers on his arrest and trial. Other material is in various Home Office papers on disturbances, communist activities and strikes.

In 1931 SS1 section of the Branch was transferred to MI5. Special Branch lost its role in dealing with communist subversion, though it retained an interest in the Communist Party generally, strikes, Irish Republicanism and other forms of political extremism.

Finding Special Branch officers' records

Records of Metropolitan Police service between 1830 and 1933 are available at TNA and so include those of Special Branch officers who retired before 1933. To find these papers you will need to know the officer's warrant number and to locate this, if you have not got it already, you will need to have a rough idea of when he joined. There are alphabetic registers of joiners, grouped over periods of time, between MEPO 4/333, covering 1830–1842, and MEPO 4/338, covering 1911–1933. The indexes are held on microfilm and, with patience, you should be able to find the officer's warrant number. Using this you can then locate, using other indexes, their Certificate of Service records, which are also in the MEPO 4 series. Do not expect the Certificate to tell you details of their work, but it will give dates of promotions etc.

The Certificate of Service for Harold Brust, confirmed as a Special Branch sergeant in HO 45/10892/357291, is in MEPO 4/470. The record does not actually say that he was in Special Branch, though it provides the various dates of his promotions. It does give some confirmation of what at first appear to be some rather peculiar stories in Brust's autobiography *I Guarded Kings*, in which he describes how, as personal servant to Sir Francis Villiers, British Ambassador in Portugal, he tackled an anarchist

Special Branch officer Harold Brust. Special Branch officers like Brust carried out much of MI5's leg work in both world wars.

assassin in the grounds of the embassy, and joined the Metropolitan Police on his employer's recommendation. It is recorded that he was Villier's servant before entering the police. Brust joined as a constable on 5 October 1908 but was posted to CID in July 1909, made sergeant in May 1913 and inspector in January 1920.

The service papers of Patrick Quinn, who headed Special Branch between 1903 and 1918, are held in a special series within MEPO 3 series for officers who served with distinction. Quinn's are in MEPO 3/2896 and include his letters of recommendation when he joined the Metropolitan Police in 1873, notices of his many commendations, details of his various periods of sickness, his letter of application and a brief physical description. Among his many commendations are one for 'his admirable conduct in a case of conspiracy to cause an explosion', dated 30 January 1897, and three involving (with other officers) 'services rendered which largely contributed to the successful issue of a prosecution for, conspiracy to commit wilful damage', dated 4 July 1913.

There is a TNA Research Guide *Metropolitan Police (London): Records of Service* available as a hard copy at TNA and online at: http://www.nationalarchives.gov.uk/catalogue/RdLeaflet.asp?sLeafletID=104.

There are a number of Special Branch policy files in TNA's MEPO files, particularly relating to increases in the Branch due to special conditions. MEPO 2/1297 covers augmentations to the Branch generally between 1909 and 1914, MEPO 2/1310 relates to increases specifically linked to suffragette disturbances and MEPO 2/1643 to increases needed to carry out aliens duties at various ports.

Special Branch files

In theory there are 182 Special Branch files held in TNA's series MEPO 38 – 'Metropolitan Police: Special Branch: Registered Files' – but, in practice, the vast majority are 'Retained by Department under Section 3.4'. The headings under which the files are grouped include: Extremism, Communism, Hunger Marches/Unemployment, Strikes/Trade Unions, Foreign Revolutionary Movements, Irish Republicanism, Naturalisation, Diplomatic and Royal Protection, Arms and Ammunition, and Foreign Criminals. Of the open files the majority cover protection (perhaps a less-contentious area than most).

One of the few files released is that of George Orwell (MEPO 38/69) which shows that as Eric Blair (his real name) he came to the attention of the Borough of Wigan police because of his associations with local Communists and 'has been making enquiries respecting local industries, Coal Mines, Factories etc, and that he is to visit a Mine in the Wigan area'. It was suspected that Blair (who also received correspondence addressed to 'George Orwell') was a writer. With hindsight we know that Orwell was working on researches for *The Road to Wigan Pier*.

Within two days Special Branch furnished Wigan police with a four-page report giving Blair's date and place of birth, parentage, education at Eton and his service with the Indian Police. Included was the note that he resigned, having 'told his intimate friends that he could no longer bring himself to arrest persons for committing acts which he did not think were wrong'. It describes his period researching *Down and Out in Paris and London*, details his living arrangements and his connection with one Francis Gregory Westrope, who 'is known to hold socialist views, and considers himself an intellectual'.

A brief report from 1937, enclosing a review of *The Road to Wigan Pier*, noted that 'Blair is now fighting in Spain with the P.O.U.M. in Bob Edward's contingent'. A January 1942 report recorded that Blair was working in the Indian Section of the Middle East Department of the BBC: 'This man has advanced Communist views and several of his Indian friends say that they have often seen him at communist meetings. He dresses in a bohemian fashion both at his office and in his leisure hours'. Notes were kept of Orwell's connections, particularly with the Freedom Defence Committee, until 1948.

Trials and cases

Special Branch officers frequently gave evidence at trials with their names reported in the press. Any case involving the Branch was likely to have been fairly high profile, so a search of the national papers should bring up reference to the officer's name.

The Branch increased in size to deal with violence resulting from the activities of the women's suffragette movement, so a search of TNA's website for papers relating to suffragettes may turn up Special Branch material.

Special Branch officers carried out the arrests of German spies during the First World War – MI5 do not have arrest powers – and gave testimony in court. Inspectors Buckley and Fitch arrested the German agent George Breeckow on 4 June 1915 and, on searching his room, found a false passport, chemicals for making invisible writing, handwritten notes on British warships and a notebook with suspicious addresses. A few days later, Fitch and Buckley arrested Breeckow's fellow spy Lizzie Wertheim. Both officers gave testimony at their trial (WO 141/3/1) and, after the war, Fitch wrote a florid account in which he vastly magnified his own small part in the case, which had been solved by MI5 with little help from the Branch.

Because Special Branch carried out many interviews and low-level investigations for MI5, a number of their reports can be found in the MI5 files, particularly those relating to domestic Communists. The files on Rajani Palme Dutt, founder member of the Communist Party of Great Britain (KV 2/1807 – KV 2/1809), contain reports from at least fifteen named officers from PCs H Bridge and B C Ravenhill up to Superintendent Canning.

Special Branch officers also reported to the Home Office on seditious, pacifist and revolutionary movements and their reports are frequently found in HO series files. There is a report from Herbert Fitch on allegations of cooperation between the Independent Labour Party, the No Conscription Fellowship, the Society of Friends and the Fellowship of Reconciliation to obstruct the Military Service Act 1916 in HO 45/10801/307402. Though he notes many close connections between the organisations and their members, Fitch is unable to prove a conspiracy.

During the Second World War several Special Branch detectives were seconded to MI5 to investigate sabotage, leakage of information and fifth-column activity. As the war progressed their initial enquiries wound down but they began investigating traitors and renegades. KV 4/165 contains a brief report on their work, naming Spooner, Burt, Davies, Skardon, Edwards, Smith and Fish as the officers and giving some details of their cases. Superintendent (later Commander) Burt left a description of some of his work with MI5 (hiding behind a cover of work for the Intelligence

Corps) in his book *Commander Burt of Scotland Yard*. Skardon stayed with MI5, becoming one of their finest interrogators, persuading Atom spy Klaus Fuchs to confess by reminding him of the debt his family owed Britain, who had taken them in as penniless refugees from the Nazis.

Indian Political Intelligence

Indian Political Intelligence (IPI) was established in 1909 following a wave of bombings and assassinations of British officials in India. Investigations revealed links between secessionists in India and groups based abroad, particularly in Britain and Canada. Superintendent John Wallinger of Bombay Police travelled to London in 1910 and established close liaison with Special Branch. Wallinger employed agents of his own in small numbers among the Indian nationalist movements in the British universities and Paris. Home Office agents in the USA provided some information, and a Vancouver Immigration Department officer ran a small operation on the American west coast. This officer, William Hopkinson, became known to the radicals and he was murdered in October 1914.

IPI files are held in the British Library's Oriental and India Office collection under the following references:

- IPI-1 Indian Political Intelligence Organisation and Personnel, 1912–1949
- IPI-2 Islam and the Khilafat Movement, 1922–1940
- IPI-3 Inter-Departmental Committee on Eastern Unrest, 1922–1927
- IPI-4 Communism: Russia, 1922–1938
- IPI-5 Communist Party of Great Britain, 1921–1948
- IPI-6 Communism: India and Indian Communist Party, 1921–1950
- IPI-7 Meerut Conspiracy Case, 1928–1933
- IPI-8 Revolutionary and Terrorist Activities, 1914–1942
- IPI-9 Control and Censorship, 1918–1949
- IPI-10 Indian National Congress, 1928–1947
- IPI-11 League against Imperialsm, 1925–1942
- IPI-12 Other Organisations and Movements, 1921–1947
- IPI-13 North America, 1912–1948
- IPI-14 Axis Powers, 1924–1949
- IPI-15 Other 'Country' Files, 1921–1949
- IPI-16 Personal Files, 1916–1949
- IPI-17 Miscellaneous Reports and Subjects, 1916–1949

IPI ran agents in Switzerland during the First World War and Wallinger watched Indian troops in France for signs of sedition, exchanging information regularly with MI5, SIS and the Foreign and Colonial Offices. He sat on the small inter-departmental committee that ran a double agent (known as X but really Victor Krafft) against German plots to subvert Indian troops in the Far East and later to cause problems in Mexico.

Though it is said that IPI ceased operating its own agents after the First World War and became dependent upon other agencies for information, there are occasional references in the IPI files suggesting otherwise. L/P&J/12/76 apparently consists of 'SIS reports on Russian positions and clandestine activities; German-Soviet treaty; Oriental Secret Propaganda Bureau, Moscow', but the markings on some of the reports – 'W E14' – suggest that they were provided by one of Wallinger's agents. IPI virtually became part of MI5 during the Second World War and was disbanded on Indian independence.

The *India Office List*

The *India Office List* is the official list of British civil servants in India and is a useful source for background information on IPI officers. The 1926 List, tells us that Wallinger's successor, John Hunter Adam, was a superintendent in the Indian Police Service (North West Frontier Province). He joined the Police Service on 22 November 1902, was promoted superintendent in November 1912 and made inspector general of the NWFP Police in November 1914. He received the OBE in June 1918, was on Special Duty in charge of the Intelligence Bureau at Peshawar in December 1919 and was deputed to England (to act as Wallinger's replacement) in February 1923.

IPI staff

The only IPI staff list, dating from December 1939, survives in the MI5 files. KV 4/127 lists a total of twelve staff, comprising Lieutenant Colonel P C Vickery and Captain V W Smith, Miss C E H Barne, Mrs S T Barne Connor, Miss Curtis, Miss Matthew, Miss Penn, Miss K D Phillips, Miss Sparrow, Miss Thuillier, Miss Wallace and Mrs D V Wilford.

The origins of secret service as we know it

The end of the Boer War saw a series of reviews and changes to almost every aspect of the British Army. Training, structure, welfare and weaponry were examined. This included intelligence.

There were a number of structural changes within the War Office (detailed in WO 106/6083 – 'History of development of Directorate of Military Intelligence 1855–1939'), with 'Special Duties' (a euphemism that included secret service) first coming under Section I3 and then, in 1907, under MO5. Former Special Branch officer William Melville was invited to work for the War Office in a private capacity. He retired from the police and established an office with the name 'W Morgan – General Agent' in December 1903. Melville recalled: 'My duties were rather vague but were generally to enquire into suspicious cases that might be given to me; to report all cases of suspicious Germans which might come to my notice; the same as to Frenchmen and foreigners generally; to obtain suitable men to go abroad to obtain

William Melville, former head of Special Branch, the War Office's chief agent 1904–1909 and MI5's first detective. He died in late 1917.

information; to be in touch with competent operators to keep observation on suspected persons when necessary' (KV 1/8). There is a fascinating file, incorporating some of his reports, in KV 6/47 – 'Miscellaneous Records'.

Another War Office agent was Herbert Dale Long, an Englishman born in Paris in 1875 and sometime resident in Brussels. While Melville dealt with matters at home or the near continent, Long made trips to Madagascar in 1900 and 1905/6, during which period he also examined points of interest in East Africa. In 1908 he went to Hamburg sounding out businessmen who might be useful to the War Office in establishing a secret-service organisation in Germany.

Spy mania

In 1903 Erskine Childers wrote his famous novel *The Riddle of the Sands* in which two Britons stumble across a German plot to invade England. It was immensely popular and created a wave of imitators, principally the writer William Le Queux. Le Queux was a hack writer of the very worst kind but his novels of British pluck facing Teutonic ruthlessness struck a chord when Germany was expanding her fleet in direct rivalry with the Royal Navy. Le Queux had some important admirers including Lord Roberts and Alfred Harmsworth, owner of the *Daily Mail*. Le Queux encouraged people to write to him about people they suspected were spies and one newspaper, caught up in the spy fever, even appointed a spy editor that readers could write to with their concerns. Under intense political pressure the Liberal Government needed to appear to be investigating reports of hundreds of spies operating in Britain. At the same time both the War Office and Naval Intelligence began to look at Germany as a potential enemy and to consider intelligence operations against her. Herbert Dale Long's 1908 mission was part of this.

In 1908 Colonel Edmonds of MO5 contacted Le Queux and became convinced of his integrity and knowledge about German espionage, taking as read his reports of suspicious groups of holidaying Germans mapping roads and railways and of sinister waiters listening to conversations. Edmonds persuaded the Secretary of State for War of the threat and in 1909 a subcommittee of the Committee of Imperial Defence examined the question. In spite of the poor quality of the evidence they agreed to the establishment of a secret-service bureau.

The Secret Service Bureau

On 26 August 1909 a meeting at Scotland Yard between Sir Edward Henry, Commissioner of the Metropolitan Police, Major General Ewart, Lieutenant Colonel Macdonogh and Colonel Edmonds of the War Office, with Captain Temple representing Naval Intelligence, resulted in an agreement to establish the Secret Service Bureau, to be split into a naval section (headed by Commander Mansfield G Smith Cumming) and a military section to be headed by Captain Vernon G Kell of the South Staffordshire Regiment. There is a copy of the minutes of the meeting in KV 1/3 and other correspondence in the FO 1093 series and WO 106/6292. Kell's letter of acceptance of his post and a copy of his curriculum vitae are KV 1/5.

Kell had a British father and Polish mother, had done intelligence work during the Boxer Rebellion and written a history of the Russo-Japanese War. He spoke French, German, Russian, Italian and Chinese. Cumming's qualifications are more of a mystery, though he was mechanically and technically adept, a good motor-car driver, a founder member of the Royal Aero Cub and qualified as a pilot in 1913.

For a variety of reasons (including a clash of personalities) the Bureau rapidly began to split along espionage and counter-espionage lines with Kell taking on counter-espionage and Smith Cumming (generally known as Cumming or 'C') foreign espionage. Both Melville and Dale Long became agents for Kell, investigating suspicious foreigners in Britain. Kell established contact with chief constables (vital for his work) and slowly began to accumulate a staff – his first clerk, Mr J R Westmacott, was appointed in March 1910, to be joined by his daughter a year later. He also acquired three more officers and another detective before the end of 1911. Cumming, on the other hand, worked alone until Thomas Laycock was appointed to assist him in 1912.

Though Kell and Cumming were supposed to share an office, they never really did so. Cumming took a flat in Whitehall Court and he used this for meeting agents, and gradually this became his headquarters.

MI5 before the First World War

The work of MI5 before the First World War was twofold: '(1) The investigation of particular cases involving a definite suspicion of espionage and (2) The construction of legal and administrative machinery calculated to embarrass, penalize and if possible frustrate such attempts in general and in the future.' (KV 1/35).

There are histories of MI5's work in KV 1 series, and these go into considerable detail about individual cases and try and paint a picture of a well-organised and well-funded German secret service at work in Britain. In retrospect, many of MI5's suspicions were founded either on wishful thinking or on German officers doing a little bit of casual 'espionage' in their spare time, much as British officers did when travelling abroad. The first proper case that Kell investigated, that of Lieutenant Helm, arrested in Portsmouth in September 1910 for sketching forts, looks very much like this. Helm was found guilty but discharged having been bound over. Through a stroke of luck, Kell's colleague Captain Stanley Clarke overheard a conversation on a train and got his first real lead into German espionage. A naturalised British subject of German origin had been approached to supply information to a F Reimers but had refused. Armed with Reimers' name and address, a watch was kept by the Post Office on mail addressed to him and a number of his other British contacts were identified. By monitoring and following this correspondence a number of other 'spy addresses' were pinpointed. When a German agent slipped up and could be arrested without revealing their correspondence was being checked, Special Branch officers, under Kell's direction, made an arrest and the spy was charged. Several agents were imprisoned and another was quietly dismissed from the Royal Navy.

On 22 August 1911 the new Official Secrets Act was passed, making the work of counter-espionage much easier. Lists of aliens were drawn up with the assistance of chief constables and through access to the 1911 Census – by August 1915 Kell had listed 30,000 aliens. Various German clubs, charities and other institutions were investigated and a list compiled of suspects to be arrested in the event of war.

By 4 August 1914 MI5 consisted of 9 officers, 3 civilians, 4 women clerks and 3 detectives.

SIS before the First World War

Though Cumming's diary (in so far as it has been published) suggests he had little to do and little success in this period, it is clear from one or two scraps of information elsewhere that he was not doing nothing. The earliest SIS report located is on Austrian shipyards and dates from January 1910. Cumming's agent is clearly a man able to access most of the shipyards in Trieste and seems to have been a businessman in the shipping industry who was posing as a purchaser. He met directors but slipped into the yards and, when caught in a prohibited area, talked his way out with the aid of a small bribe. He later discovered, however, that his room had been 'turned over'. He provided detailed information on the yards, their equipment and facilities, workers and ships they were building. At one point he crawled under a tarpaulin to measure the calibre of some guns.

Cumming also took over the running of some agents from the War Office, including an Austrian codenamed 'B' who spied on Germany but would not spy on his own country. Attempts were made to establish an office in Brussels (the hub of European espionage as spying was not illegal there) under Herbert Dale Long. Cumming's close association with Naval Intelligence involved him with attempts by NID agents to gather information on German coastal defences. Captain Regnart (Royal Marines) sent Lieutenant Vivien Brandon and Captain Bernard Trench to Borkum. They were arrested and served prison sentences and Cumming later had to fight off attempts by Regnart to take over his operation.

A businessman and Royal Naval Reserve officer, Richard Tinsley, who ran the Uranium Shipping Company in Rotterdam, was recruited to run a station in Holland. A small network of agents was established along the German border to act as a trip-wire against a sudden German attack.

Chapter 3

MI5 IN THE FIRST
WORLD WAR

On 4 August 1914 MI5 directed police raids across the country and, it was stated by the Home Secretary in the House of Commons that 'no fewer than twenty-one spies, or suspected spies, have been arrested . . . some of them long known to the authorities to be spies'. Following this announcement, MPs passed the Defence of the Realm Act (DORA), giving sweeping powers to the authorities.

MI5 had greatly contributed to the drafting of DORA, compelling all aliens to register and restricting their movements, allowing censorship of mails and telegrams, restricting travel abroad and incoming visitors and allowing for vetting of individuals. It was an important part of MI5's armoury against German spies and responsible for the gradual throttling of attempts to get information out of Britain, but its passing by Parliament was based on a dangerous fallacy. Analysis of the records shows that the only German spy arrested and prosecuted was Karl Gustav Ernst, a naturalised German barber who had acted as postmaster for the German network before the First World War, who MI5 had long known about. The MI5 Game Book (KV 4/112) is quite clear. Most of the 'spies' arrested in August 1914 were guilty of little more than being vaguely foreign and were released. But the myth of the breaking up of a major espionage ring stuck and contributed greatly to MI5's reputation.

Throughout 1915 increased restrictions were placed upon aliens, with the internment of Germans of military age and repatriation of many more, some long resident in Britain. Later MI5 drew up a Grey List of people who had naturalised or had a foreign parent, and many were banned from work in official or sensitive positions.

Between August 1914 and the end of the year a further 23 Officers and 35 civilian staff were recruited to MI5. By October 1917 it had 91 officers, a small force of detectives, 227 military ports police and 360 clerical staff. In 1916 all the sections that came under Kell's control became known as MI5, the name by which the service has been known ever since.

The Germans had decided, before the war, that they would employ visiting agents who would travel to Britain, send reports by telegraph or mail and return to the continent to be debriefed. Thanks to MI5's list of 'spy addresses', the Censorship Department was able to intercept some messages and advise MI5 that German agents were at work.

First caught was Carl Lody, a former ship steward who could pass as an American. He entered Britain in August 1914 but wrote to known 'spy addresses' and his mail was intercepted. He was traced and arrested, revealing several other contact addresses. Lody was tried by court martial in open court at London's Guildhall and sentenced to death, though his demeanour and courage greatly impressed the press and public. He was executed by firing squad at the Tower of London in the early hours of 6 November 1914.

Other German agents followed and in early 1915 German records show that some twenty were in the country, though MI5 were on the trail of many, tipped off either by the Censorship Department or by Richard Tinsley, SIS officer in Holland who watched the spy addresses there. As their names, cover names and methods became known MI5 created files on them. If an agent was suspected, but nothing could be proved, they were turned away at the ports and placed on a Black List, which was circulated to consuls and military control officers abroad so that these individuals could not obtain visas.

Kell's detectives had other successes. In early 1915 letters in invisible ink were intercepted en route to Holland. They were replaced with fakes containing false information. The spy, Karl Muller, was traced and tried in camera at the Old Bailey. His original letters were used in evidence against him and he was shot secretly in the Tower. MI5's Major Hinchley-Cooke continued to send false information for over a year after Muller's death and received his salary and expenses, totalling nearly £400.

After the Battle of Jutland faked photographs of damaged British ships were passed to the Germans under Muller's name. Later, a plan was hatched to trap a U-boat by sending details of the sailing of an important steamer. The U-boat surfaced, to face a waiting destroyer, but managed to dive and escape. The Germans now became suspicious and Muller was 'given an official burial' (KV 4/16).

Probably not 'The Muller', but Major Drake and Captain Maxwell of MI5 are obviously enjoying their drive, in spite of Government exhortations not to use cars for pleasure! (from the MI5 cartoon book *Secrets of Waterloo(se) House*).

Hinchley-Cooke used Muller's pay to buy a two-seater Morris car for official use. Nicknamed 'The Muller' and driven by a uniformed woman chauffeuse, it was stolen, in broad daylight, from outside MI5's office in Charles Street in 1918, and was never recovered.

Further successes followed, with the arrest and execution of another ten spies during the course of the war. Other suspects were interned under DORA. German intelligence began to struggle to get agents into the country after the end of 1915, when the introduction of the Military Control System meant that entry visas became harder to obtain. Attempts to use American journalists as spies seemed successful at first, but the arrest of George Vaux Bacon and his sentence of death (commuted) and the turning of one of his colleagues, Roslyn Whytock, by British agents in New York, ended that. By 1918 the Germans only had a couple of agents in Britain.

Records of German spies

MI5 records of only a couple of spies caught during First World War have so far been released. KV 2/3 relates to Leopold Vieyra, a spy of Dutch origin

Carl Lody, the first German agent captured by MI5 in the First World War. He was shot in the Tower after an open trial at the Old Bailey, but his obvious patriotism and bravery greatly impressed the British public.

who was sentenced to death in 1916 (reduced to ten year's imprisonment) for passing naval intelligence to Germans in Holland. KV 2/4 and KV 2/5 are George Vaux Bacon's files. There are other files (KV 2/1 and KV 2/2) on German agent Mata Hari, executed by the French in 1917, and KV 2/6 to KV 2/10 on Irish patriot (or renegade depending upon your viewpoint) Roger Casement, caught by the police and executed in 1916.

Fortunately for researchers, other records of the period that have been released contain much information. There are records relating to Hans Lody's trial in DPP 1/29, HO 144/3324, WO 141/82, WO 32/4165, WO 141/82 and WO 71/1236. Lody was as popular in Germany as he was with the British public and enquiries were made about his execution and place of burial after the war (WO 32/4159 to WO 32/4164).

Lizzie Wertheim was a German-born woman who had married a naturalised Briton, from whom she was estranged. An independently wealthy socialite, she may have been an MI5 suspect for some time before she was contacted by visiting agent George Breeckow in 1915. They became lovers and she toured Scotland obtaining naval information for him. Arrested and tried, George was executed but Lizzie was sentenced to ten year's penal servitude. By 1918 she had been committed to Broadmoor suffering with delusions and died there in July 1920. Her Home Office file (HO 144/7269) deals with her mental condition and the power of the Public Trustee to pay for her maintenance in Broadmoor from her estate. Both files were only released in 2005. Her trial, along with that of George Breeckow, is detailed in DPP 1/30.

File HO 144/1727/277302A is the Home Office file on Karl Muller's accomplice John Hahn, convicted at the Central Criminal Court on 11 May 1915 for attempting to communicate information to the enemy. This file was only released in 2007. Using TNA's search engine it should be possible to find other Home Office, War Office and Director of Public Prosecution files on individuals. If you are unable to find anything then a Freedom of Information request to the relevant department might prove useful.

By the end of the war MI5 had caused 65 people to be convicted of espionage or treason, had 226 interned, 25 persons subject to restrictions, 650 removed, restricted or excluded from certain areas, recommended 354 aliens for deportation and had 422 people arrested on a variety of charges such as distribution of seditious pamphlets, incitement to strike, incitement to sabotage, spreading false war news and abusing the royal family (KV 4/114).

Other MI5 work

The investigation and arresting of spies was the glamorous part of MI5's work but its main role was the prevention of espionage. The registration of aliens (and subsequent internment and expulsion of Germans and Austrians) was part of this, as well as giving advice to government departments on the vetting of staff. MI5 took over port security with port-control officers stationed at all major harbours. Huge amounts of information were collected by the police, armed forces and SIS and collated and analysed by MI5 (h), which issued reports on wide-ranging matters. The June 1918 report survives in KV 1/51 and contains files on, among others, the following: Preventive Policy and Measures, Passports and Travel, British and Allied Suspects, Neutral and Enemy Suspects, Peace Propaganda and Scotland Yard interviews. Among the Allied suspects are a W B Shearer, 'all round crook and card sharp'. MI5 checks against him discovered he was a known associate of a suspected enemy agent and the American authorities said he had been posing as an American intelligence officer. He was deported to New York with a 'No Return' permit.

MI5 Ports Police

In 1916 the Military Foot Police (Port Section) was established to work in conjunction with MI5's port-control officers. Known as 'Greencaps' after their distinctive green cap covers, over 300 were employed on security and counter-espionage duties. These involved not only guarding ships, suspects and dockyard equipment, but conducting interviews, searching ships and suspects and even some following of suspects and working in plain clothes. The force was composed of junior NCOs unfit to serve abroad. Their service records (those that survived the blitz) are likely to be in WO 363 or WO 364,

Name.		Corps.	Rank.	Regtl. No.
DOWLE		MFP	L/Cpl	P/3406
T. W.				

Medal.	Roll.	Page.	Remarks.
VICTORY	MFP/10/32	289	
BRITISH	do	do	
STAR			
Theatre of War first served in			
Date of entry therein			

The medal card for Lance Corporal Dowle of the Military Foot Police. Only a couple of hundred of the thousands of Foot Police served with MI5, so the MI5 Staff List in KV 1/59 will need to be checked if you are trying to find out if an individual Foot Police officer was part of MI5.

which are available at TNA on microfilm and online at Ancestry.com. KV 1/22 contains a detailed report on their work.

MI5 records from the First World War – the KV 1 Series

Most of MI5's records from 1904 to 1919 are held in TNA's KV 1 series, and some of them predate the foundation of the Secret Service Bureau. When the KV 1 records were first released it was explained that they were the only files surviving from the period, but a few personal files have been subsequently released in the KV 2 series, mostly because investigations continued into the 1920s. Thousands of records on people the service had looked at, but who had been proved to have no connection with the enemy, were destroyed after the war.

The files are a mixed bunch, compiled after the war for illustrative and historical purposes by a special team who left a brief history of their work, as well as short autobiographies, in KV 1/53.

Unfortunately TNA's online catalogue does not break down the contents of the various Branch report appendices and annexures, as these frequently provide copies of documents, details of procedures, lists of military control officers, who were frequently SIS officers (in KV 1/30), and some interesting cases that did not lead to espionage charges.

The earliest records (KV 1/1 to KV 1/12) cover the setting up of the Secret Service Bureau, some of Vernon Kell's diaries, brief financial accounts and a memoir by William Melville, describing his early work for the War Office.

There were various changes in Branch designations as MI5 developed from MO5g in 1914 and gradually expanded and took on more responsibilities. The final organisation, at November 1918, consisted of six branches, each divided into sub-sections.

MI5 branch reports

A – Control of Aliens

Though MI5a was formed in 1917, the origins of its work went back to the influx of Belgian refugees in September 1914. Careful checks had to be made on refugees applying for work in the munitions industry. MI5 employed Belgian officers to carry out its work.

In March 1916 the staff was transferred to the Ministry of Munitions as Ministry of Munitions Labour Intelligence (MMLI), soon known as Parliamentary Military Secretariat 2 (PMS 2). The staff and work transferred back to MI5 in 1917.

D – Imperial Overseas Intelligence

Created to deal with espionage cases from the colonies and Ireland, D branch monitored Home Rule movements in India, Ireland and Egypt, pan-Islamic movements and Greek Royalist movements receiving German support. Liaison was maintained with civil and military authorities throughout the Empire. An MI5 officer established the Eastern Mediterranean Special Intelligence Bureau in 1916, covering the Middle East, North Africa, the Balkans, Persia and Turkey. Records of D Section are in KV 1/15 to KV 1/19, but these are copies of memoranda on their contacts and the establishment of security bureaux abroad.

G – Investigation of Espionage

The investigation reports in KV 1 are a disappointment for anyone looking for details of how investigations were carried out. Records deal purely with the agents that MI5 identified and captured, not with the many German agents investigated, identified and prevented from coming to Britain or interned under DORA. There is no mention of which MI5 officers carried out individual investigations or any detail of how they decided which way to proceed. There is usually an indication of how the German agent was identified.

There are few details of the numerous investigations carried out by MI5 with the cooperation of the police and other authorities into suspects that were subsequently cleared, though it is obvious from one or two of the appendices to the reports that there were very many of these.

E – Control of Ports and Frontiers

Holland, Spain, Denmark, Sweden, Norway (and until 1917 the USA) were all neutral and there was considerable traffic with them and Allied countries. German agents based in, or travelling through, neutral states were reaching Britain and a sophisticated system of controls was introduced. Created in May 1915, MI5e coordinated operations, confirming when permits to travel to Britain could be granted. It received reports from SIS agents worldwide and from Allied intelligence services and compiled MI5's Black List of suspect individuals, addresses and companies. MI5e ran the port-control officers and ports police and liaised with Special Branch and customs officers.

MI5e's records within KV 1 are extensive, including histories of the Branch, theoretical papers on methods of control, histories of controls in various ports, a history of the ports police, details of how alien seamen were controlled, notes on techniques used to avoid the control, reports on control offices abroad and copies of various regulations, documents and forms.

F – Prevention of Espionage

The prevention of espionage was MI5's 'core business' and MI5f coordinated policy with other Government departments over such matters as dealing with aliens, passes and permits, legislation, precautionary measures and vetting. Many of its staff members were lawyers. Its records are in KV 1/35 to KV 1/37.

H – Administration

The basis of good intelligence work is a strong and capable administration and MI5h provided the filing, typing, look-up of Registry records, personnel support and the whole multitude of bureaucratic back up that a modern organisation depends upon. In August 1915 H Branch had a staff of

8 officers (including a woman, Miss E A Lomax) and 59 clerks. By September 1918 this had grown to 15 officers and 68 staff.

Procedures were written for all the clerical processes, including filing, looking up references, movement of records and the carding of details of individuals for ease of looking up. Using these procedures it is possible to work out fairly exactly what kind of daily routine and duties someone you are interested in was doing.

There are a couple of sections of MI5 history conspicuous by their absence, at least in terms of released documents. Section G1 carried out investigations into pacifism and undesirable political parties, partly on the assumption that they were receiving German finance. A history of G1 was never written, and details of its work have to be gleaned from working through the released files on individuals. There are also no histories written (or at least released) on the Indian or Irish Sections of G Branch that later became D Branch.

Tracing MI5 staff

There is a detailed list of MI5 staff arranged in chronological order in KV 1/59. This gives dates of employment and in most cases the general type of work carried out, i.e. clerical staff, port policeman or messenger. MI5 employed a large number of domestic staff such as lift attendants, chauffeurs, washerwomen and cleaners. Officers are notable by having their names spelt out in capital letters. This list will confirm a relative's employment and dates they served, but not the section they served with.

KV 1/52 is a separate list giving snapshots of the staff of the various sections throughout the war. With diligent searching, it is possible to find the section that an individual worked in and from there a section history and description of the work done. Miss S M Humble joined MI5 on 30 April 1917 as a clerk. She worked for G2a section responsible for 'Examination of suspicious letters and cables and irregular methods of correspondence and evasion of censorship' (KV 1/57). KV 1/46 gives a general description of the type of work she would have done and KV 1/48 (Chapter XIV) a history of G section at the time. MI5 worked closely with MI9 the Censorship Department and there are interesting files on their work in KV 1/73 and KV 1/74.

MI5 officers

Most of Kell's officers were just that – Army officers, many of them having been invalided home from the Western Front. There is likely to be a file on

MI5g officers photographed on Armistice Day to celebrate the end of the war. A few officers can be identified. Front row, centre: Lieutenant Colonel Sealy Clarke, far left: Lieutenant Colonel G M Ormerod (probably), fourth from left: Commander F B Henderson; middle row: third from left: Captain S J Sassoon (cousin of Seigfried Sasson), sixth from left: Sir Herbert Thirkell, eleventh from left (fourth from right): Captain S R Cooke, twelfth on left: Major W A Alexander; back row: second on left: Lieutenant N Randall, far right: Lieutenant F H Hawes. (with grateful thanks to Dr Nicholas Hiley)

their Army service previously, with an occasional reference to work done at MI5, in the WO 339 and WO 374 series. The work they were engaged in can be discovered by using the staff lists in KV 1/52. There were a number of Indian Civil Servants (ICS) who joined MI5 throughout the course of the war, possibly because they had experience of intelligence or police work already. Robert Nathan, for example, had previously investigated terrorist activity in Bengal and broken up a gang there in 1907. Details of their previous service in India can be found in the Indian Civil Service List. A small number of RNVR officers worked in MI5 and their service records are in ADM 337.

Charles Blanchet – MI5 double agent and officer

Charles Blanchet (WO 374/7075) was an MI5 officer who joined the service in 1917.

Unusually (though not uniquely) Blanchet was originally foreign, a Swiss

Most officers' files will contain a protection certificate giving basic details about them and the last unit served with. Captain R G Berner is shown as serving in MI1c – cover name in the First World War for SIS.

man who had naturalised in 1915 (HO 144/1412/276052) to join the British Army. He was married to an English woman and had worked in London for her father for some years. He became a private in the Army Service Corps and was posted to France, where he was recruited by Colonel Kirke of the Intelligence Branch to act as an agent in Switzerland. Blanchet had been a

Swiss Army officer, so was experienced in military matters. In return for this service he was promised a British commission on his return.

> He behaved with great pluck, and went into Germany after having offered his services . . . to the German Consul in Switzerland. He was detained for several days by the German secret service and put through a severe interrogation, with a view to establishing his bona fides . . . so severe an interrogation, indeed, that he felt sure that they had discovered that he was a 'double agent'. The Germans appear to have omitted the obvious precaution of making enquiries about him in Switzerland where he is well known, and where they would easily have discovered the fact that he had joined the British Army.

Blanchet returned to Kirke once the Germans were satisfied he was genuine and was debriefed. A note in Kirke's papers at the Intelligence Corps Museum show that Blanchet had been promised a job in the Censorship Service. Kirke sent him to Britain to work under MI5, where he was looked upon him with great suspicion 'thinking that the Germans were pretending to have been hoodwinked and that he was actually in their pay'.

Blanchet proved to be absolutely straight, giving MI5 'considerable valuable information about German methods, identity of their chief agents . . . and has also worked very satisfactorily in maintaining spy correspondence, under our instructions, with the German secret service'.

The double-agent operation ended in late 1916 and Blanchet had interviews with Major Carter of MI5g and William Melville and was commissioned a Lieutenant in the General List and employed in MI5g.

Blanchet remained with MI5 during the staff reductions of 1919. On 31 December that year he was one of only ten officers still serving in G Branch. He was finally demobilised on 1 June 1920.

Major T H Howard – MI5g

The MI5 Staff List (KV 1/59) shows Major T M Howard (4th Battalion, Hampshire Regiment) serving with MI5 between 5 August 1918 and 7 February 1919. KV 1/52 puts him in G3, listed as dealing with correspondence and communications with Allied military missions, as well as 'Special investigations into the cases of suspected persons in diplomatic, financial and political circles'. Surely a sensitive area indeed for anyone to investigate? The December 1918 *Army List* does not show any T M Howard, but there is a Major T H Howard (4th Hampshires) seconded to the War Office. This then is our man and his file is WO 374/35028.

Medical reports show Howard had been suffering from neurasthenia, loss of memory, delusions and hallucinations, and the Army Board considered him unfit for active service. His Wimpole Street doctor stated 'it is quite clear that he possesses a nervous system . . . quite unable to stand any kind of strain. Under pressure he soon displays a number of serious lapses of memory, strong phobias and even delusions. . . . he is quite unfit to take up any such duties again although I hope he will go on all right if he lives a perfectly quiet life'. Howard was determined to do his bit, resisting attempts to have him removed from the Army, insisting he was fit for home service. He spent most of the war at the Hampshire Regiment Depot before his brief service with MI5. He was still serving in the Army in 1920 and went to Berlin employed by the Reparation Commission.

Major George Pepper – MI5's Quartermaster (WO 374/53419)

Major George Pepper became MI5's Quartermaster when the service was taking on the ports police and numerous uniformed staff. The KV 1/59 Staff List shows he joined on 28 July 1916. KV 1/52 shows George was serving in Section H7 and his duties are explained, in detail, in KV 1/53/3.

'H7 is in charge of the interior economy, of the subordinate personnel and all the stores and supplies.' Duties included checking the boiler room; inspecting toilets, supervising charwomen, ensuring the Girl Guides dusted bookshelves and tables, visiting the cook and ensuring waste paper was correctly collected and incinerated. George maintained a close relationship with MI5's suppliers and was in charge of garaging the motor cars. Under him was the chief clerk, responsible for logging all post, keeping the address book up to date, looking after petty cash and paying the orderlies, cooks, cleaners and drivers.

George Pepper was born in 1855, served as a private in the 99th Foot in the Zulu War, becoming sergeant major, then honorary major and quartermaster with the Wiltshire Regt. He retired in 1910 and in August 1914 was working as assistant secretary to the Surrey Territorial Association. In 1916 he was persuaded to join MI5, where he stayed until March 1922, when he retired for the second time.

On his appointment with MI5 the War Office argued against paying him a major's salary, saying he was nothing more than a glorified clerk and, on the assumption that his salary with the Territorials had only been £150 pa, had agreed to pay him £200 pa, plus a uniform allowance. This was slightly less than he was already earning but, as Kell pointed out, 'he accepted the terms out of a spirit of patriotism and in his anxiety to do his bit'. It was assumed his time with MI5 would count towards his pensionable service.

In 1921 Pepper told Kell that he had worked for six years on a reduced salary, with no increase since 1916. He pointed out he had been forced to live on his original Army pension without any supplementary pay. Kell explained to the War Office that Pepper had worn a uniform and performed 'military duty' but they insisted he was a civilian clerk for pension purposes. The War Office section dealing with civilian employees did not have him on their books and said that, as he appeared in the *Army List*, he must be an officer. Kell used this as the basis of seeking a pension increment. He pointed out that Major Pepper was serving under the Army Act 'and if he had misbehaved himself, or indeed if he does misbehave himself in future I should have, and certainly shall, try him by Court Martial. Under these circumstances how is it possible to accept that he is not rendering Military Service?' The War Office fell back on their original definition of Pepper's duties as being 'purely clerical work' as the basis for their refusal. The Director of Military Intelligence weighed in: 'Major Pepper's work has been co-equal with that of any Regimental quartermaster combined with the administration of highly confidential and technical work connected with the special branch of my directorate . . . he has administered and controlled the military personnel both at Headquarters and the ports'. Pepper's duties 'entailed his being responsible for the pay and allowances, discipline, demands for and the replacement of clothing and equipment for all the NCO's and men attached to MI5 . . . He was, in fact . . . carrying out the duties of an Adjutant and quarter-master'. At the end of May 1921 it was agreed that a reassessment of pension could be allowed 'as a special case'. When he retired in 1922 he received a pension of £419 10s pa.

Following Pepper's death in October 1925, Kell was approached by his widow, whose pension had reduced to £70 pa, and wrote to the War Office: 'I understand that the death of her husband has left her in very straitened circumstances . . . Major Pepper served in MI5 for 6½ years from 1916 to 1922 and on leaving us had a total length of service of 50 years. I do not know whether it is possible for you to augment the ordinary rate of pension in this case, from any source, but if so, I should be very glad to recommend such a proposal . . . this is a case which well deserves sympathetic consideration'. This time the War Office stood their ground and until her death in 1936 Mrs Pepper had to live on her widow's pension, supplemented by small sums from rents, dividends and grants made by service charities and the War Office Relief Fund. Every year she completed a statement of income and expenses to the War Office.

Detectives and agents

It is not clear whether all Kell's detective staff are listed in KV 1/59 or not – certainly their chief, William Melville, is along with one J Regan, who left MI5 in August 1916 and is clearly marked as 'Deceased', and H I Fitzgerald, who is simply marked 'left' with no leaving date. C Tartellin is listed as a detective between December 1915 and July 1919 and A J Regan (possibly related to J Regan?) between September 1916 and June 1919. P A Whittome served between November 1916 and July 1919. Detectives are carried as a quite separate section of Kell's accounts (KV 1/11). In the February 1919 accounts there are separate entries for both 'informants' and 'agents' (KV 1/12). It is these people who are the hardest to trace and that MI5 have done their best to conceal, though a few can be brought out of the shadows by looking further into Kell's accounts earlier in the war. The April 1915 accounts lists the initials W M, J R, H F, W B, de V and J W as being paid, but gives no further details. The accounts for July 1915, however, detail: Meville

A Christmas card showing a suspect undergoing interrogation, 1918. By this time MI5 had reduced German espionage activity in Britain to virtually zero. (with grateful thanks to Dr Nicholas Hiley)

W and Regan J (obviously the two detectives mentioned earlier), along with Fitzgerald H, Burrell Wm, de Vos A, Winkelman J and Hailstone F. In December 1915 they are joined by someone known only as Emil and C Tartellin. Presumably these were either other detectives or agents, though the exact nature of their roles is unspecified.

Women workers in MI5

The first woman employed by MI5 was Miss D Westmacott, daughter of Kell's existing clerk, recruited in January 1911 as a typist; a secretary,

Miss H M Newport, was employed in October 1911. By August 1914 there were three female clerks and one woman typist. With the outbreak of war the volume of work increased dramatically with up to 2,000 suspect files a month being created. The clerical staff increased in line with the work so in December 1916 there were 161 female employees; in December 1917 there were 245 and in June 1918 there were 296. MI5 had a fairly advanced employment policy for women – they had the first woman in charge of departmental finance (1916), a woman (1917) ran their photographic section and two sisters managed the printing department.

The Electric Bells having broke, the G.G.'s (*not* Grenadier Guards) sit outside Maj. D.'s door in case he wants them.

A group of Girl Guides wait outside Major Drake's office. Girl Guides and Boy Scouts were used as internal messengers within MI5, having been sworn on their honour not to look at the files they carried. (from the MI5 cartoon book *Secrets of Waterloo(se) House*)

As well as clerical roles, women were employed as lift attendants, drivers, housekeepers and body searchers at ports. Girl Guides were used as office runners and the departmental doctor was female.

The filing of documents called for attention to detail and scrupulous following of procedures. Every detail of a suspect had to be noted separately in case only one of them came to MI5's attention again. A report in KV 1/53 notes:

> We actually have a subject card headed WOODEN LEG and another headed FALSE NOSE. A man whose chief claim to distinction was that he was in possession of a copy of the 'Hymn of Hate' can be traced under that heading, while we have even a card headed DONKEY due to the fact that the only noteworthy statement in a certain report was that someone's donkey was 'acquainted with the Rathbone family'.

Recruitment of female staff was at first done by word of mouth among existing employees, but as the need for specialist staff grew (for example Russian speakers) discreet approaches were made to the principals of various ladies colleges such as Cheltenham Ladies College and Somerville

College to recommend former students. Many of the lady staff of the bureau served in Paris, New York, Rome and Egypt in MI5's branches there, taking their valuable experience gained at home into these foreign offices.

There is a list of female staff who received distinctions in KV 1/50, and sixteen women are recorded who were mentioned for their services in the *London Gazette*. Miss E A Lomax received both the MBE and, later, the CBE for her work. Some of the female staff who served abroad in MI5 were put forward for the War Medal and there is a list of these also in the appendices of KV 1/50.

MI5 and the police

Much of MI5's day-to-day interviewing and low-level investigation work was carried on by either Special Branch in London or by liaison officers with the county and borough forces. There are occasional references to these officers in the police committee minutes of local councils, which you may find in your local county record office, but generally these simply record officers as being engaged in work for the War Office. Exeter Constabulary noted that work for the War Office required one of their detectives to work on secondment to them almost full time.

There is a list of the MI5 liaison officers in HO 45/10892/357291 – 'Appreciation of work done by police officers for M.I.5' – which was sent to the Home Office indicating which officers, below the rank of chief constable, deserved recognition. In Exeter Kell singled out Detective

Celebrating MI5's August 1916 move from Watergate House, 15 York Buildings, Adelphi to Waterloo House, 16 Charles Street, Haymarket. Vernon Kell stands at the front while Majors Dansey, Haldane (in spurs) and Drake lead the way followed by an assortment of MI5 officers and staff. (from the MI5 cartoon book Secrets of Waterloo(se) House)

THE BIG PUSH.

WHERE ARE WE ALL TO GO? OR, THE INVASION OF THE NEW OFFICE, 1916.

Inspector William Henry Hall; in Norfolk four officers, Superintendent Edward Woddeson, Superintendent Welcome Basham, Inspector Webb at Cromer and Sergeant Percival Levick. Most county forces have three or four officers named and the larger borough forces more than this – Newcastle upon Tyne has nine names and Liverpool eight, with four officers in each port commended for their assistance to the port-control officer.

Other domestic agencies

Competent Military Authorities

The Defence of the Realm Act (DORA) gave unprecedented powers to the Army and Navy through appointed 'Competent Authorities' who were authorised to open mail, tap telephones and to watch generally for suspicious behaviour. Each Competent Naval or Military Authority (CNA or CMA) could delegate their powers so that a considerable number of people were empowered to snoop on their fellow citizens. It is difficult to assess the scale of their operations as not a great deal seems to have survived. Certainly each large Army garrison had an intelligence officer who reported to War Office section MT1(b), later HD3, and every large naval base had an officer who reported to NID in London.

MT1(b) circulated intelligence résumés, none of which have survived in the War Office records. As the Royal Flying Corps was part of the Army, the copies circulated to it were passed in 1918 to the newly formed RAF and survive in the AIR 1 series. AIR 1/550/16/15/27 – 'Home Defence Intelligence Summaries: Aliens, etc' – contains these reports for late 1914 and early 1915. These reflected the paranoia of the times perfectly – Army officers visited properties owned by Germans or German companies, pronouncing that they had been built specifically as artillery platforms in preparation for invasion, concealed Zeppelin bases were looked for and strange lights and the movements of suspicious cars were tracked. Railway employees were instructed to report on suspicious travellers and detectives (presumably from the civil police) watched stations. It is clear that aliens were being watched and informed against by civilians, and that some civilians were employed by the Army for conducting searches, as well as acting as organised 'observers'. The reports continue until the end of 1916 in various AIR 1 files, but by then most German aliens had been interned or repatriated and the intelligence officers turned their attention to publicans serving soldiers in uniform and, more worryingly, to anti-war organisations and individual pacifists. Very few direct reports on the actual enquiries made by the CMAs survive, though KV 2/2256 on Russian Navy officer Nicholas Wolkoff does have some papers on an investigation begun by the local CMA into an alleged German spy – who turned out to be Wolkoff – the Russian naval attaché! MI5 had a low opinion of CMAs and their investigations.

In addition to MI5, MT1(b)/HD 3 and the police, an extensive postal censorship organisation was put in place for both incoming and outgoing mail. CMAs also had the power to have mail censored and seem to have used it. Though there are numerous files relating to the theory and practice of censorship, including two files on the history of the postal censorship department MI9c (DEFE 1/445 and DEFE 1/446), the day-to-day files of the censorship department seem to have been destroyed. The only papers I have located are in the Jersey Archives (references A/E/1 and A/E/2) and contain correspondence between the Censor, the Governor's Office and the Aliens Control Office. The Censor monitored correspondence of Jersey's small German and alien community, including monks and pensioners, and launched a number of investigations by the police and military.

ADM 131/20 – 'Plymouth Station: Correspondence' – contains some reports relating to spies, lights and investigations carried out by the Competent Naval Authority in Plymouth in the early part of the war.

Another unofficial organisation that provided information to the Special Branch was a network run by theatrical impresario and businessman Arthur Maundy Gregory. Though he was never an officer, he applied for a commission (WO 339/124709) and asked for a job in the secret service. He cited in his support that he had run an information-gathering organisation for Special Branch using his agency. Neither MI5 nor SIS was interested in him.

The stay behind agents

One of Kell's early tasks was to 'mark down spies and agents in peace and to remain in German lines and spy on troops if they land' (KV 1/1). A possible extension or development of this may be the 'Observer Scheme', established by Home Intelligence MT1(b) in late 1914 (AIR 1/550/ 15/15/27). In 1910 Kell sent Herbert Dale Long to join the Legion of Frontiersmen (a patriotic organisation to bolster the defence of Britain and Empire). He visited Brighton, Ipswich and Yarmouth finding suitable men. Kell also interviewed Captain Hely:

who has been acting unofficially as Intelligence Officer along the

N E Coast defences . . . He appears to have a good knowledge of
what would be required in time of war, and to have got in touch with
a number of people along the east coast, as far south as Whitby, who
might be useful to us some day.

Dale Long submitted a report on his return from the east coast in which he
suggested various individuals. Kell wrote: 'Nos 1, 2, 3, 12 and 14 might be
worth noting. I shall enter them among my "likely agents".'

MT1(b)'s observers are difficult to disentangle from Kell's agents as
sources of information on both are scarce. The east-coast observers reported
to MT1(b) on Zeppelin raids (AIR 1/550/15/15/27), but were they
intended to do more than this? No lists of either the War Office observers or
Kell's agents appear to have survived.

PMS2

There was a massive expansion in the munitions industries during 1915 and
with newly (or poorly) trained employees working flat out with flammable
and explosive material, there were accidents, sometimes very serious ones.
In the prevailing mood many of these were ascribed to German saboteurs.

The Ministry of Munitions Labour Intelligence (MMLI) was formed in
February 1916 from a nucleus of staff from MI5. It was quickly renamed
Parliamentary Military Secretariat 2 (PMS2) to disguise its intelligence
function. Their principal work was checking for foreign saboteurs but they
rapidly expanded into investigation of strikes and industrial arrest. It has
been alleged that a network of PMS2 *agents provocateurs* created fictitious
reports of dangerous German influence among left-wing shop stewards and
also pretended to have uncovered a plot to assassinate the Prime Minister,
David Lloyd George. Certainly the prevailing mood of the authorities was
almost hysterical when it came to supposed German plots. Following the
conviction of a group of anarchists from the Midlands with plotting to kill
Lloyd George with a blowpipe dart and serious allegations that *agents
provocateurs* had been involved, PMS2 was wound up and monitoring of
sedition and strikes returned to Special Branch, while registration of aliens
employed on munitions work returned to MI5.

There are no surviving PMS2 files in the Ministry of Munitions series
(MUN) but a few records survive in early KV 2 files where they
corresponded about industrial unrest and socialism. There is a report on
PMS2's work in KV 1/13A, a memorandum on the duties of PMS2 sections
in KV 1/13C3 and a list of PMS2 staff in KV 1/13H.

Chapter 4

SIS IN THE FIRST WORLD WAR

The war began well for SIS. Though bound up with other more formal papers in FO 371/2159 for August 1914, a brief note survives to Sir Edward Grey, on Foreign Office headed paper and dated 31 July 1914, reading:

> One of our agents arrived from Cologne this morning & reports that troop trains are moving through there on their way to the western frontier. This confirms what Mr Lambton(??) told me this morning that though Germany haven't issued decree of mobilization she is really mobilizing – French Govt think that Germany wishes to incite the Paris Cabinet to issue mobilization decree first and to give France the appearance of being the aggressor.

Whatever else Cumming had achieved as head of SIS, this was one of his main tasks carried out – the trip-wire system had worked.

According to what has been published of Cumming's diary he spent much time over the next few weeks trying to establish networks on the continent. On 2 August he agreed with Alfred Rothschild to 'arrange for a large sum of £ in Brussels, which G G can call for' (excerpt from Cumming's diary, published in Alan Judd's *The Quest for C – Mansfield Cumming and the Founding of the Secret Service*). Presumably G G is Lieutenant George de Goldschmidt, recorded in FO 371 as being in Brussels, along with veteran agent Henry (*sic*) Dale Long, Captain J A Cuffe RMLI and Demetrius Boulger: 'These persons are all employed by the Intelligence Department of the War Office'. They may be the men who recruited British nurse Edith Cavell into SIS. One of her biographers claims that at this time she was visited by two Englishmen, who subsequently left the city in a hurry. Long left SIS in early 1915, possibly following the German discovery of material he had left in his mother's flat in Brussels. It is believed that he joined the Intelligence Corps from the Army Service Corps on 21 January 1918 and served in Le Havre.

Cumming visited Brussels in August, as well as Paris and spent much time sending agents to neutral countries such as Switzerland and Holland. His chief man in Holland was Richard Tinsley who ran his networks out of the offices of the Uranium Shipping Company, and who had close connections with the Dutch police, many of whom were suspected of being in his pay. Tinsley's networks supplied a vast amount of valuable material on German troop movements in Belgium and on blockade running by smuggling through the Netherlands. He also watched German espionage headquarters in Holland and provided MI5 with much vital information.

Cumming also sent an intelligence mission to Russia under Captain A N Campbell (who had previously worked for Kell) to liaise with Russian intelligence. With him went Lieutenant Stephen Alley, a fluent Russian speaker who was to play a prominent role in future events in that turbulent country, and who was still serving (as a senior MI5 officer) in the Second World War. Campbell was recalled because he clashed with the naval and military attachés and made reports of a political nature that upset the ambassador. One or two of his reports can be found in the FO 371 papers for late 1914 unmarked as being SIS sourced, but carrying Campbell's name.

In late September Cumming was in France visiting his son Alistair who was with the Intelligence Corps. They were driving back together at night when their car came off the road, killing Alistair and putting C in hospital for about six weeks. He lost a leg, which was replaced with a wooden one.

WO 339/7419 is Alistair's record and there is a copy of the telegram sent to his mother dated 4 October 1914, which reads: 'Deeply regret Lieut A Smith Cumming Seaforth Highlanders, died the result of a motor accident on 3rd October, his father Commander Cumming was severely injured and is in French hospital at Meaux. Lord Kitchener expresses his sympathy.' Although Cumming tried to work from his hospital bed, it seems likely that his immediate absence from the centre of events may have been the reason that the War Office created other intelligence networks of its own. Majors Cecil Aylmer Cameron and Ernest Wallinger (brother of John Wallinger of IPI) established networks running into Belgium from Folkestone via Holland and over the next three years there were clashes over agents and areas of responsibility.

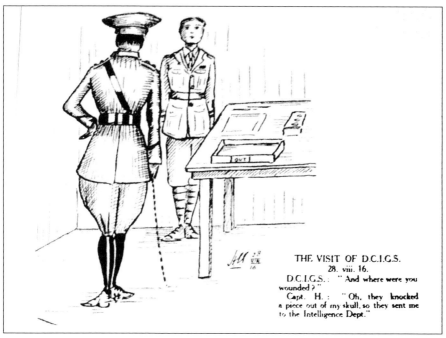

THE VISIT OF D.C.I.G.S.
28. viii. 16.
D.C.I.G.S. : " And where were you wounded ? "
Capt. H. : " Oh, they knocked a piece out of my skull, so they sent me to the Intelligence Dept."

As casualties mounted it was common practice for both MI5 and SIS to employ officers wounded at the front in their headquarters. At least some people had a sense of humour about it! (from the MI5 cartoon book *Secrets of Waterloo(se) House*)

In 1915 Cumming's agents went to New York (Sir William Wiseman arrived there in October) and into Spain. Information on troop movements continued to come out of Belgium and reports on conditions in Germany came in from SIS representatives in surrounding neutral countries. Agent 'Walrus' reported from Berne on 17 September that in Leipzig 'Labour is becoming scarce and materials are lacking. Everywhere there is a fear of tomorrow. The winter campaign is anticipated with dread, and the Russian victories, which were expected to finish the war, not having done so already there is but little enthusiasm. The correspondent is convinced that, if the Allies continue the blockade for some months, they will attain their end.' In autumn 1915 bread rationing was introduced around Berlin and price controls imposed on a wide range of foodstuffs.

The author Compton Mackenzie joined SIS in 1915 and went to Athens to do counter-espionage work. He was recruited by Lois Lort Samson, a former Levant consul who had been running agents against Turkey since

February 1915, working under cover of a refugee relief fund. Though he struggled against the apparent absurdities of secret-service work, Mackenzie did a good job, identifying German agents, working closely with his French colleagues and running an agent inside the German Legation.

One triumph of 1916 was obtaining details of damage to the German Fleet after the Battle of Jutland. Tinsley's agent R16 had access to the main German shipyards and some of his reports are in ADM 223/637 – 'Agents' Reports: Naval'. Station Chief N1 reported from Copenhagen on 19 June 1916 that 'German agent D15 just arrived from Wilhelmshaven bringing document proof of visit there' and set out a three-page report detailing damage to German ships, casualties, estimated repair times and accounts of the battle from the German side. A week later R16 reported via Rotterdam 'In accordance with instructions received from you on June 2nd I went at once to BREMEN, travelling from there to DANZIG, KIEL, ROSTOCK, GEESTEMUNDE, EMDEN and to SANDE near WILHELMSHAVEN in order to ascertain the exact German losses in the North Sea action of May 31st.' R16's five-page report confirms many of D15's details, listing eight ships (possibly nine) that were going to be out of service for at least three months. Naval Intelligence graded the report as 100 per cent. Another successful operation obtained information on numbers of U-boats under construction by getting details of reinsurance contracts made by Germany with Swiss insurance companies.

In 1916 the Military Control System was introduced. To stop the movement of German agents military officers were posted to all the European capitals, with smaller offices at most of the major ports and borders. To travel to an Allied country, passports were required and were usually granted for one trip only. The Military Control Officer (MCO) could refuse leave to travel or contact London, where MI5e would grant or refuse it. MCOs reported to both Kell and Cumming but, being based abroad, came under Cumming's command and received their communications via MI1c (as SIS was now being known, having been theoretically subsumed into the War Office organisation). Even Allied subjects, who could not be refused travel, were obliged to report to the MCO who would check their credentials and secretly mark their passport to indicate his opinion.

Compton Mackenzie was made MCO in Athens and, having set up a similar system, was able to offer much sound advice and a memorandum written by him is in FO 372/936.

In 1916 Cumming appointed Conservative MP Sir Samuel Hoare head of his Russian Intelligence Mission. Hoare received training in the arts of espionage but his role was more political, keeping the various factions within the mission focused on transmitting military and naval intelligence from the Russians, working with them on the economic blockade and training them in cable censorship. By the end of 1916 there were persistent rumours that a Peace Party under Rasputin's influence was involved with Germany and plots started against him. Hoare was approached by one of the plotters, and told that a plan existed to murder Rasputin. Hoare may not have been aware, but three of the mission's officers, Captain Scale, Oswald Rayner and Stephen Alley (now MCO), were closely involved with the murderers and Rayner may have been present at the killing. Certainly he was involved in the tidying up operations afterwards.

In 1917 the Russian revolutions took place and Greece entered the war on the Allied side. In the latter case this meant that the SIS organisation could emerge from the shadows and begin to assume formal duties. As a result many SIS officers can be identified through searches in the FO 286 series. FO 286/638 reveals that Commander J L Myres RNVR took over as Military Control Officer in Athens and lists many of his staff and agents.

Myres's organisation ran postal and telegraph censorship, as well as counter-espionage and passport control. George Georgiadis was one of his secret agents. There was confusion between SIS and Naval and Military intelligence who sought to take control of SIS's functions. As a result there are minutes of meetings and lists of staff. Among the many names are Lt W C Mountain, Captain Mark Astley Shute, Lieutenant Commander H O Whittall, Lieutenant E Knoblock and Lieutenant CH Tucker RNVR. Even some of the female office staff are named, including Miss Woodley, Myres's secretary, and Miss Bossy, his shorthand typist.

The Russian revolution of October 1917 began the long war between SIS and the Russian Bolsheviks. Determined to try and keep Russia fighting British officers from the various agencies in Petrograd and Moscow tried first to persuade Lenin and Trotsky to stay in the war, then to plot against them. By August 1918, as British troops landed at Archangel, plans were in hand to suborn the Russian Fleet and to buy off Lenin's bodyguard in preparation for a coup d'état. Their plans failed and various SIS officers found themselves imprisoned. C's organisations in Belgium and France helped to provide vital information during the final year of the war in watching the movement of German troops in Flanders.

Within days of the Armistice C's agent S8 (journalist Clifford Sharp) was in Berlin reporting on conditions there. After the war SIS agents watched for German attempts to circumvent the blockade, which continued until the signature of the Versailles Treaty, and for attempts to avoid the treaty's terms.

George Georgiadis – an SIS agent in Greece

The political situation in Greece made life difficult and sometimes dangerous for British agents, even though they were working in an Allied country. Rivalries between the Monarchist (pro-German) Party and the Popular (pro-Allies) Party could result in arrest and mistreatment. Georgiadis family legend says George acted as a British agent in Greece and that three of his children died of disease while he was serving in Patras. Fortunately for the family, records of his service and what befell him and his family are preserved in TNA FO 286 series ('Consulate and Legation Greece General Correspondence'). There is also material alluding to his secret service in his naturalisation papers (HO 144/6272).

George was born in Kastoria, Macedonia, in 1881, part of the Turkish Empire. Educated at the Government Commercial School in Athens, he lived in the USA between 1905 and 1908, after which he went to Manchester as an importer and exporter of textiles. He married a Welsh girl, Ellen Morris, and they had six children. In 1914 he studied at Birmingham University before becoming a teacher in Cyprus. Being in Cyprus at the outbreak of war entitled him (it was thought) to exchange his Ottoman Turkish nationality for Cypriot-British, which he did in 1917. During 1917 he was appointed British telegraph censor in Syra. Struggling to support his growing family on his small wage, he was appointed agent of the White Star Line at Messenia, where he resumed his old fur-trading business. This was cover for secret-service work on behalf of Lieutenant Tucker, the British Passport Officer at Patras.

George was ordered to report to Tucker on: all local suspects, movements of enemy agents, submarines and coast signalling, rumours, sedition, local politics and enforcement of passport regulations. He was warned:

> Your value to us as an agent can only hold so long as you are not suspected of being in our service, and it is only fair to warn you that should we hear from any other sources that you are in our employ, your payment and employment will cease without notice.

Tucker ensured the Greek authorities knew that George was engaged in secret work for their ally but did not tell the French Consular Agent Monsieur Keck, as he was not trusted. Greek factionalism and inter-Allied lack of trust, along with personal interests of the consular officials, combined to throw George's mission into disarray and caused him material and personal loss and great emotional upset.

The identity card issued to SIS agent George Georgiadis by his chief Charles Tucker in 1918. (with grateful thanks to the Georgiadis family)

The family proceeded to Kalamata on 19 March 1918 and George began sending his reports to Tucker. On 17 May he was arrested by the police who refused to allow him to refer to the British Consulate. The police searched his home, scattering his furs and confiscating his papers. Under threats of violence, Georgiadis handed over his confidential papers. He was held in prison overnight but, though released, was closely watched and not allowed to leave town.

It became clear that Monsieur Keck had arranged for George's arrest and denounced him as a German spy. The Greek authorities, who were Monarchist and anti-British, had connived in his arrest and deliberately denied him access to British officials.

Following her husband's arrest, Mrs Georgiadis, without access to his codes, telegraphed Lieutenant Tucker in Welsh to try and explain what had happened. Enough was intelligible to the Englishmen at Tucker's office to prompt them to make enquiries. Tucker was unable to get a satisfactory answer from the Greek authorities in Patras and the officers holding George refused to allow him to leave Kalamata. A couple of days after his release he was arrested again and this time taken to Athens. He managed to get a message to Patras and Athens, but on his arrival he was put into solitary confinement and fell seriously ill. He later wrote to Tucker: 'What I suffered in that prison I neither can, nor would I like to attempt, to describe. The result was that I became ill and cought (*sic*) for a long time afterwards.'

In desperation his wife wrote to the British Legation in Athens:

Today I have telegraphed to you stating the miserable plight we have been left in; among strangers, knowing little of the language, four little children (the) eldest being six years old, the youngest two babies of four months. Three weeks ago our little girl three years of age died here, and all the remaining children are in a bad state of health indeed.

Georgiadis was imprisoned for eight days before Lieutenant Mountain managed to get him released to Patras, where he was taken in by the British Vice Consul. When Tucker returned he ordered Georgiadis to return immediately to Kalamata in order to impress upon the locals his innocence and to demonstrate that he had full British approval and authority. At Kalamata he was faced with tragedy. In addition to his daughter Theadora, who had died earlier, his little girls Rose and Lily had died in his absence.

In 1920 the Greek government finally paid compensation for the damage done to George's furs at the time of his arrest, and two Scotland Yard officers personally handed over a cheque for £315 9s. In 1924 George applied for naturalisation as a British subject. His naturalisation papers are in HO 144/6272. Even if his other papers had not survived, the application documents would have confirmed many of the stories that the family had been told.

CX

By the end of 1914 SIS introduced CX as an indicator of SIS-sourced material and as a marker on all its messages. An agent was told 'If you have urgent material you want to get to us quickly put CX CX CX CX on the report'. Thanks to these identifiers, which gradually came into common usage, it is possible to identify agent reports that can be used to verify (or cast doubt) on aspects of received SIS history. From early 1915 onwards CX reports begin to appear from SIS representatives throughout Europe confirming they were in Copenhagen, Christiana (now Oslo), Berne, Lausanne, Athens and Bucharest, as well as Petrograd. During 1916 CX reports were filed from further afield, i.e. Portugal, Albania, New York and South America. A report from Valparaiso dated 17 April 1916 discusses Chilean attitudes to the war, including allegations that the admiral at Punta Arenas had aided the German Far East Squadron in 1915 and the cruiser *Dresden* when she was hiding off the Chilean coast.

Though in most cases, where an agent is identified at all, they are usually only shown by a codename, based on the initial by which their controlling SIS station was known, e.g. D2 as Danish agent 2 or S50 as Swedish agent 50, or sometimes by a single name such as MAURICE, very occasionally the name of the individual is given. A report from Geneva dated 28 December 1918 clearly names a Monsieur Paul Esterhazy as providing information about Russian banking transactions running into several millions of francs. Other CX does occasionally give the name of the SIS officer transmitting or receiving it. An SIS note to the Foreign Office dated 29 November 1918 says that 'For your information, the attached instructions have been sent to our representative in Stockholm'. The attachment, marked CXM 877, is addressed 'DMI for Scale'. Major John Dymock Scale was assistant military attaché and ran an extensive network of agents (all prefaced with the initials ST) out of Stockholm into Russia, Finland and the Baltic.

A partial list of CX identifiers can be found in Appendix 6 of this volume.

Finding CX material

CX sent to the Foreign Office should have been filed in Red Jackets, making them easy to locate and remove before they were sent to the Foreign Office library. There was a breakdown in procedures early on, so that some CX was entered in Green Jackets and some in plain jackets. When Miss Paget took over the filing of Red (SIS), Green (Secret) and Blue (Wireless intercept) papers for the Northern Department of the Foreign Office in 1924 she was 'horrified' to discover that some CX was being filed as Green. She immediately changed procedures to ensure that all CX was stored correctly in future, and that Green papers were checked for CX before going to the library.

No attempt was made to locate previously misfiled CX so it has been released into the public domain. The card indexes don't give any clues that a paper or file is SIS sourced, though there are occasional references to SIS reports, with file numbers, in the early years of the bound indexes in the 1920s. Unfortunately most, if not all, of these files have not been released.

Other CX material turns up in Admiralty (ADM) and War Office (WO) files, and there is a lot on German arms production in the Ministry of Munitions files (MUN). A prime source is the KV 2 series as MI5 relied on SIS to report on suspects abroad and to investigate foreign intelligence services. The vast amount of CX in the KV files is both a blessing and a curse – a blessing because it is there at all, a curse because it is likely to produce a skewed view of SIS activities. Reporting on foreign intelligence organisations was only a small part of SIS work, so the material should only be treated as a special case, not used to generalise too extensively.

Counter-Bolshevism officers

At the end of 1918 the threat from Bolshevism prompted SIS to establish a network of counter-Bolshevism officers in some smaller European capitals, working with the knowledge and cooperation of their police and governments. From the surviving records in the FO 371 series it is impossible to say how long the network of officers continued, but counter-Bolshevism CX was still being generated at the end of 1920 and turns up in various KV 2 files.

Among the officers listed (FO 371/3951) were:

Captain K E Lawrence	Christiana (Oslo)
Captain G W Tait	Lisbon (relieved by Lieutenant V G Chancellor RNVR)
Captain G D Williams	Madrid
Lieutenant Davidson	Stockholm
Major Langley	Berne
Mr S C B Wood	The Hague

Chapter 5

FINDING FIRST WORLD WAR INTELLIGENCE SERVICE RECORDS

The Intelligence Corps, MI5, and MI1c were part of the Army, though in the case of MI1c this was nominal only. This means that there are often records of their officers' service in the officers' personnel files of the War Office. These are held at TNA in their WO 339 and WO 374 series.

There are two main series of service records. If you do not know which your officer was, try both series.

- WO 339 series contains nearly 140,000 records for officers who were pre-war regulars, temporarily commissioned in the regular Army or commissioned into the Special Reserve;
- WO 374 series contains nearly 78,000 service records for officers given either a Territorial Army or a temporary commission.

Both series can be searched using the surname but be aware that with a common surname this might take some time. There is a microfilmed index in WO 338 which is an alphabetical list of officers that will give you the reference you will require. TNA's website and paper guides at Kew give hints that might help to speed up your search.

Intelligence Corps officers

Intelligence Corps officers' records give rather more information about where they went and what they did than the average officer serving with an established regiment or corps. This may be because there was no organisation other than the War Office itself to administer their records. If the exact nature of their work is rarely recorded, you can usually trace their movements and try and make deductions.

RNVR officers' service records

The Royal Naval Volunteer Reserve allowed men with an interest in the sea, but who were not in the Merchant Navy, to join the Royal Navy as a reservist or in time of war. Many officers required for the intelligence services because of their specialist knowledge of languages, code-breaking or technical matters were enlisted in the RNVR. Most of the officers who served in Room 40, the Admiralty code-breaking section, many of the military control officers and even a few MI5 officers served officially in the RNVR, at least as far as the administration of their pay was concerned.

The RNVR officers' records (ADM 337) consist of microfilmed ledgers that have been indexed online so that officers can be searched for by name. The records of service are generally brief, giving full name, date of enlistment and name and address of next of kin. There are usually details of the work the man undertook and of his postings. The vast majority of RNVR officers served on small boats or in shore stations but those who served with SIS can generally be recognised because they are noted as being on 'special service outside the Admiralty under DID', or a variant of this.

There is a brief mention, in the form of a memo from MI1c to MI5 in KV 2/1953 (Fritz Joubert Duquesne, a South African suspected of sabotage), of a Lieutenant D'Oyley Carte working for MI1c in December 1917. Rupert Doyley Carte's record is in ADM 337/123/203. It shows that he joined the RNVR (unpaid) as a temporary lieutenant on 13 March 1917 for 'Duty outside Admiralty (N.I.D.)'. Next of kin was his mother, Lady Dorothy Doyly Carte of Eyot House, Weybridge. His commission was terminated on 1 January 1919. There is no direct mention of his working for MI1c.

The record of another of Cumming's officers, William Barclay Calder (ADM 337124/148), notes that he was 'Military Control Officer, Murmansk'. However, generally you will have to dig further to find more information. The Foreign Office card index is a good place to start.

The Fleet Air Arm Museum at Yeovilton holds a series of ledgers setting out the calculations for RNVR officers' war gratuities. Though there is usually little more information in these ledgers than in the usual service record, they can be useful in the event that there are gaps in the records elsewhere.

The service record for William Barclay Calder RNVR, an SIS man in North Russia where he worked as a military control officer.

SIS officers

Captain H Jump MI1c

Captain H Jump's file is thick with MI1c references (WO 339/6850). The file is stamped CX 063796, which also reveals his SIS connections.

Captain Henry Jump, 1st Royal Dragoons, was wounded and captured near Ypres in 1914. His unit had held out for four days and while attempting to reach his commanding officer, Jump was hit in the thigh. Unable to move, he had stayed behind when his squadron was forced to withdraw. He remained a prisoner until repatriation in November 1918. A medical board classed him as 100 per cent disabled but MI1c sent him to Switzerland as an assistant military attaché to 'work in liaison with the Swiss General Staff and MI1c'. He was in Berne as a passport-control officer and was 'handling Eastern questions'. In 1920 he was seconded to the Foreign Office 'in view of his special knowledge of eastern affairs as handled in Switzerland'. He was described as 'expert on oriental questions concerned with the military situation in Egypt, India etc.'.

Jump retired in 1921 and applied for his war and wound gratuities. MI1c had, unfortunately, ruined his chances of a wound gratuity and he was not entitled to as much of a war gratuity as he thought. His Army service was deemed to have ceased when he was seconded to the Foreign Office so his gratuity was £200 lower than expected. His wound gratuity had to be claimed within five years of the wound but by going to Switzerland he had missed the deadline and 'It is regretted therefore, that your application for compensation in respect of your wound of the 30th October 1914 cannot now be considered'.

Captain T S Laycock – the tragic death of an ex-SIS officer

Captain T S Laycock appears on a diagram of the Directorate of Special Intelligence (October 1915) as being in MO6c, responsible for secret service under the Director of Secret Service. His service record is WO 339/13678. His file is a thick one and examination reveals why – pension problems caused by the irregular way he was recruited. The result was not positive, and the end result tragic.

Laycock's record confirms his work for SIS before and during the First World War. Born in 1875, he had enlisted under an alias into the Militia in 1892 and transferred to the Royal Artillery in 1894. He had been promoted regularly and served during the Boer War with the Special Ammunition Column, being wounded in action in January 1902. For most of his service he had been known as Tom Laycock but in 1912, by deed poll, he became Thomas Spencer Laycock. He had taken private French lessons, passed the Schoolmaster's Course and courses in administration and was noted as 'a very good clerk'. In 1912 he had retired at his own request to work for Cumming as his first office assistant. He had been commissioned on 5 August 1914 and continued in SIS.

During the First World War he had been posted to Russia in November 1915 and served as assistant military attaché in Bucharest in 1916 (where he'd also been military control officer). He had left SIS in April 1918 to serve with the Provost Marshall's Department, and been awarded the Military Cross, as well as Russian and Romanian medals.

In 1920 Laycock tried to obtain an additional pension to cover his service after he had 'retired' in 1912, but met a brick wall. The War Office advised

Details of Tom Laycock's service record showing quite clearly that he worked for the secret service.

that 'the period you spent in the Secret Service from 1912 to 1914 cannot reckon as pensionable'. This was despite Cumming writing:

> He carried out his Duties entirely to my satisfaction and rendered valuable services to the War Office. For a considerable time he was my only assistant, and I could not have carried on without him. If it is possible to grant such a favour I consider that it is thoroughly well deserved.

Nothing was forthcoming, though Laycock managed to get a previous promotion recognised and a small amount of back pay.

Laycock committed suicide on 10 February 1927 but, as he had not been a regular officer or reached the rank of warrant officer class I before retiring in 1912, Mrs Laycock was not entitled to a widow's pension. Attempts to claim a retrospective disability pension on grounds that he had suffered mentally as a result of war service failed. Laycock's doctor certified that he'd 'become nervous, irritable and very moody, whereas previous to 1914 he was perfectly calm and even tempered. . . . this change which culminated in his final act must be attributed to his experiences in the war'.

The Woolwich Records Office sent Mrs Laycock a copy of her husband's service record showing that on 15 December 1912 he had been 'Discharged at own request'. On 5 August 1914 he had been 'Appointed to a temporary commission as Lieutenant, General List'. No mention was made of his work for Cumming between the two dates. An officer who had known Laycock intimately noted 'he would have stoutly resented that his manner or actions prior to his death suggested any mental trouble, though it was fairly obvious to most of his friends'. Mrs Laycock was not deterred and deliberately referred to his secret service in her correspondence. Unfortunately, by 1927 Cumming was dead and the bureaucracy was not inclined to bend the rules. She was bounced between the War Office and Ministry of Pensions, receiving occasional gifts or loans from the War Office Special Fund and the British Legion. She was eventually given a grant of £200, part of which was an interest-free loan, to establish a boarding house.

Jesuit priest, Naval Intelligence officer, SIS officer and agent – Pierre Marie Cavrois O'Caffrey

Alan Judd's *The Quest for C* mentions 'the little known Air Section at 11 Park Mansion in Vauxhall Bridge Road under Lieutenant O'Caffrey . . . thought to work out the courses of German bombers from intercepted radio signals . . . they probably dealt with spying on German airfields'.

The hunt for Lieutenant O'Caffrey was fascinating. A search under 'Caffrey' on TNA's website produced: AIR 1/305/15/226/157: – 'Naval Intelligence – reports and papers from Lieutenant P.M.C. O'Caffrey, R.N.V.R.'. This was a good start. An unsigned, undated memorandum states:

> Lieut O'Caffrey – a Jesuit Priest – was given a commission in the Royal Naval Volunteer Reserve soon after the outbreak of the war, for the express purpose of obtaining information solely connected with air matters in Belgium, he being particularly fitted for this task, having lived many years there amongst the people and talking like a native.

O'Caffrey withdrew his application for a naval chaplaincy, saying that he had discussed this with His Eminence, Cardinal Bourne of Westminster.

O'Caffrey was based at Folkestone and boarded steamers from Holland, interviewing refugees and collecting information which was passed to NID and the commander of the Royal Naval Air Service at Dunkirk. 'His information has proved unusually correct and has also been of considerable value in drawing up plans for our air raids'. He describes how, with help from a naval captain and 'some special inspectors from Scotland Yard', he had gathered information on Zeppelin sheds, aerodromes, factories, artillery batteries and trenches. The Belgian Surete offered to find him reliable agents to go to Belgium to obtain more information. He proposed the 'employment of certain agents known to him who were able to travel within Belgium at a cost of about £30 per week' and in February 1915 the Director, Air Department, wrote to Commander Samson, Commanding Officer at RNAS Dunkirk, confirming O'Caffrey had been attached to NID but that he 'will continue to forward reports direct to you as heretofore'.

O'Caffrey is mentioned several times in Samson's memoir *Fights and Flights*. On 2 September 1914 O'Caffrey had visited Lille in civilian clothes, spotting about 1,000 troops. He arranged with a local lawyer to provide information and began his first espionage ring when he 'started a boy scout service . . . We provided them with a bicycle and paid them 1 franc a day . . . on one or two occasions these boys brought us valuable information'.

AIR 1/562/16/15/64 Pts. I & II – 'German aerodromes and airship sheds in Belgium and Northern France' – provided intelligence reports, many signed by O'Caffrey, headed NASF (Naval Air Service Folkestone), including maps, plans, movements of aircraft and vehicles and even photographs of Zeppelin sheds at Evere and Berchem Ste Agathe, with descriptions of their construction. RNAS Dunkirk mounted several raids against them during 1915.

O'Caffrey's service record in ADM 337/117 confirms his service in NID. In 1918 he had been with the British Naval Mission to Greece and been demobilised there on 26 June 1919. He had been 'Brought to the notice of the Secretary of State for War for valuable services rendered in connection with the war' and was 'not required for appointment as assistant Passport Control Officer'.

The Society of Jesus had been unable to trace him in their records, even in the register of deceased Jesuits. At that time it was remotely possible he was still alive, but when a second attempt produced the same result, in spite of their kind searches, I was almost at a loss.

BERCHEM ST AGATHE - According to our sources of information the sheds here have not been made use of for a considerable time, and no machines have been seen on the aerodrome for at least two months. The Belgian information is believed out-of-date.

BRASSCHAET - This remark applies also to information re BRASSCHAET -(vide N.S.S. 51 13.2.15 and N.A.S.F. 54 21.2.15)

No mention is made in the report of several new aerodromes which are being prepared by the Germans far behind the lines in the centre of the country at LEEUW-ST-PIERRE, CORBEEK LOO, and LOKREN (vide N.S.S. 58 8.2.15, N.S.S. 59, N.A.S.F. 62).

No information is given in the Belgian report, concerning the suppoy of petrol, benzine, and hydrogen, which would have served to confirm or rebut that already gathered here on this subject.

--------oOo--------

A report circulated by Lieutenant O'Caffrey commenting on Belgian reports about German aerodromes and Zeppelin sheds.

Further checks on TNA's website produced a record I had previously missed: HO 144/3470 – 'Nationality and Naturalisation: Cavrois O'Caffrey, Pierre Mary, from France. Resident in Athens. Certificate 11,186 issued 30 May 1924'. The record was closed but it seemed worth an attempt to have it opened. TNA replied that the record was subject to a: 'Section 23 exemption: this section exempts information that is directly or indirectly supplied by, or relates to, certain organisations dealing with security matters such as the security services, the Government Communications Headquarters (GCHQ), or the special forces.'

They confirmed they had contacted the relevant department to see if it could be opened. I explained everything I then knew about his work for NID and SIS, that his name was already in the public domain and that several files naming him and describing his work were already open. I hoped this would speed matters up but instead received further emails saying TNA were still waiting for permission to open the record.

I suggested, jokingly, that perhaps there was some kind of scandal that they wished to keep hushed up, and searched further through the open records to see what else I could find. I found correspondence in the Foreign Office records for Greece in the 1920s. The Athens Legation described him in April 1922 as 'an Irishman named O'Caffrey', the buying agent of the Levant Mineral Company in England, who the Legation thought was in the pocket of the French. Further checks produced references to a document in 1923 not on the file – it was marked 'Missing when weeded 22/7/52' – but the file header remained, and here was the scandal! According to the file header, O'Caffrey married on 27 September 1919 and was in possession of 'a British passport, obtained for him by the Intelligence Department, in which he is described as a British subject born in London' (FO 372/2029).

Later records refer to him depositing his possessions at the Athens Consulate in 1940 and the *Navy List* shows he went back into the RNVR that year and worked again for NID, ostensibly as an interpreter. By 1945 he was a lieutenant commander posted to HMS *Nile*, HQ of the admiral commanding the Eastern Mediterranean.

On 1 February 2007 (I made my FoI request in June 2006) it was agreed a partially redacted file could be released. In spite of several redactions, it is possible to add more details to both O'Caffrey's career and his personal life.

In 1923 the Athens Consulate discovered O'Caffrey was not really a British subject so not entitled to his British passport. Questions were raised about the validity of his marriage. O'Caffrey admitted everything but said that the passport had been given to him by the British Intelligence Service. The Foreign Office liaised with MI5 and a note remarks 'MI5 have weaved a tangled web around this man and we can't get him out of it'. To qualify for naturalisation O'Caffrey would normally have to spend twelve months resident in Britain but MI5's Major Phillips suggested:

> the Department of the War Office concerned would be prepared to employ O'Caffrey again on work in Greece and though this would have the primary object of qualifying him for naturalisation. Major Phillips said he was certain the 'job' would be a 'pukka' one.

The file is redacted at this point, but a note on the cover says 'Transmit copy of letter from MI5 who intend to employ applicant on special duties in Greece'. It is not clear what O'Caffrey did on 'special duties' but by early 1924 there was movement on his application.

His memorial explains:

My full name is Pierre Mary Cavrois O'Caffrey. The latter part of my name (O'Caffrey) under which I am commonly known, is the original name of my family which is Irish in origin. Cavrois is the French form of the same name. My father only used the name O'Caffrey as a 'nom de plume' and I am the first in my family to revive it. I was born at Calais, Nord, France on 20th March 1876. On 27th September 1919 I married Miss Bilio Chryssoulis whose father was a colonel in the Greek army.

No mention at all is made of his having been a Jesuit priest! He gives details of his previous residences in Britain and the Empire and his service to the Crown, including his intelligence work.

I served first at Folkestone then (from July 1915) in London (where) I organised and managed the Air Section of special intelligence. From February 1917 to August 1917 I served in the Near East. . . . stationed successively at Syra, Samos and Mitylene.

He had then worked in security and examination in various Greek islands, ending the war at Piraeus. Three testimonials testify to the nature and quality of his work. A note in support of his application says: 'Lt Commander O'Caffrey held a commission in the RNVR from September 1914 until June 1919 and was employed by us on special duties from 1916 to 1920'. The remainder of the note is redacted but, even though the paper is headed MI5, it's signed by Lieutenant Colonel S G Menzies of MI1c, the War Office liaison section with SIS.

O'Caffrey's naturalisation was granted on 30 May 1924, with MI5 acting as go-between to the very end, sending the Home Office his final cheque by way of settlement.

First World War medal cards – a useful tracing aid

Researchers into First World War soldiers will be familiar with the card index of medals awarded to soldiers and others who served abroad under the War Office. The original index cards are now held by the Western Front Association and are available online through Ancestry.com but copies of the front of each card (the bit that holds the useful information) are available both as microfilm at TNA and as downloadable copies at TNA website. The whole collection has been indexed and can be searched online for individuals, but the same search engine can also be used to try and find whole groups of people.

The medal card for Herbert Dale Long shows that after service with the Army Service Corps he transferred to the Royal Fusiliers – sometimes used a 'cover' by Intelligence Corps men.

Searching the index under MI5 produces thirty-one records, most of them relating to women clerks who served abroad with intelligence missions or the intelligence centres MI5 ran in British possessions such as Malta. The card for Florence J Wookey notes she did clerical work at the British Military Mission, Rome. Other cards unfortunately just note that the lady was on 'Intelligence Duties'. As with all search engines, there are a number of tricks you have to be aware of, mainly to do with the various mistakes made in the indexing of the cards. While MI5 brings up thirty-one records, M I 5 produces another one and M15 another twelve.

As part of the combined intelligence effort against the Germans a joint intelligence headquarters was established in Paris, where the Allies exchanged information. The British section was known as Mission

Major Robert Eric Peebles' medal card, which clearly shows a period of attachment to MI5 from the Royal Engineers.

Anglaise, Bureau Central Interallie (BCI) and using various combinations of these words, a search produces some thirty-two of its staff.

As there is no central list of officers and men of the Intelligence Corps, the medal card index is possibly the only way of finding the majority of men who served in it. A search reveals 1,377 names.

'Military Intelligence' used as a search term brings up twenty-three people, including General Sir George Macdonogh, Director of Military Intelligence; 'Special Duties' reveals two men, Richard B Hirsch even noted on his card as being 'Special Duties – Civilian – Specially Employed by MI1c, France, Portugal and Spain'. There are no references specifically to Hirsch in the Foreign Office indexes so perhaps this one reference is the only available one to show his secret-service connections.

The civilian medal book (WO 329/2353) also lists two men serving with MI5 who are not in its KV 1/59 Staff List. Mr F C B Wood is described as 'Antwerp & Netherlands under MI5 WO 1914–1918' and Mr B H Dobson is described as 'Lent by India Office to WO in October 1915 under MI5 (o) WO 1915–1919'. MI5 (o) does not appear on any structure charts or histories for the period, so presumably this is some kind of error, though an MI5 (o) was in existence later, covering overseas possessions.

Using 'Belgian Agent' as a search term produces some 451 names and 'French Agent' only 5, and there were considerably more than this. 'French Agents', however, brings up another 263 and 'Belgian Agents' another 3,434.

Belgian and French agents

There is another source of information on the French and Belgian men and women who were employed as secret agents. Shortly after his appointment as a coordinator of the networks being run out of Antwerp, Captain Henry Landau was approached by the Belgian organisation known as La Dame Blanche – 'The White Lady'. Their emissary, known only as St Lambert, suddenly announced 'There is one condition however; they insist on being enrolled as soldiers before they commence work'.

Knowing the War Office would be extremely unlikely to agree such a request, Landau quite simply lied and promised that they would be. La Dame Blanche went on to provide vast amounts of information, particularly on German transport movements, which was passed through

La Dame Blanche was one of SIS' most productive networks providing information on German troop movements in Belgium. This map shows the key positions used by agents to record the details of train movements which were then smuggled across the border into Holland.

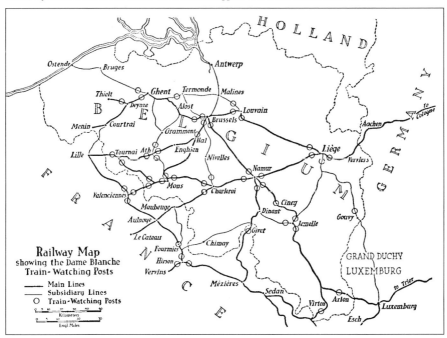

to Holland by secret couriers. After the Armistice, Landau went into Belgium to liquidate the organisation, draw up a list of members, arrange pensions for the families of executed agents and to ensure that all money had been paid. He was forced to admit his lie but promised to 'move heaven and earth with the British authorities to make good their word to their followers'. In the event, with the intervention of 'C' himself, the Army Council agreed that the agents were entitled to medals, and a roll was produced. There is a copy of it in FO 371/3758. It lists agents, in alphabetical order by surname, detailing forenames and town of residence. Unfortunately there are no further details of which parts of the organisation they worked for or what they did. It includes people who had died.

Their awards were gazetted in the *London Gazette* in August and September 1919, so it is possible to trace details of the awards through the *Gazette* online. Medal cards can be traced through TNA's online search engine: http://www.nationalarchives.gov.uk/documentsonline/medals.asp.

Chapter 6

NAVAL AND MILITARY INTELLIGENCE IN THE FIRST WORLD WAR

In the years before the First World War Naval Intelligence established a network of stations throughout the world reporting on shipping movements. Many of these were at British consulates and there is considerable correspondence in the FO 371 series.

Admiral Reginald 'Blinker' Hall (son of the first director) was appointed Director Intelligence Division (DID) in late 1914. With enormous sums of Admiralty money at his disposal and a worldwide organisation, he turned NID into Britain's biggest intelligence organisation, working closely with SIS, MI5 and Special Branch. Because SIS did not have an established organisation in the USA or many neutral countries until later in the war it was NID that worked against German influences in many places until SIS was able to take over from them in 1916 and 1917. Naval attaché to the USA, Captain Guy Gaunt ran secret agents inside the German Embassy in Washington and thwarted plots to sink Allied shipping, blow up munitions factories and foment strikes in American industries important to the Allies. As late as 1918 Hall was running agents deep into Soviet Russia in cooperation with SIS.

Because Hall had money and was closely linked to SIS (Cumming even once describing him as his senior officer) many SIS officers wore the uniform of the RNVR and their service records are noted as being on 'special service outside the Admiralty under DID'.

NID records from 1914 onwards are in ADM 223 series but they seem sparse for the First World War. There are rumours that Hall had many of them burned when he retired in 1919 to go into politics.

Admiralty Room 40

Naval Intelligence's greatest contribution to the First World War was through its code-breaking section, known as Room 40 because of its location in the Old Admiralty building. It was created, in October 1914, by Admiral Oliver, Hall's predecessor as Director of Naval Intelligence, who gave intercepts from a German radio station to the Director of Naval Education Alfred Ewing, who had a private interest in cyphers. Ewing recruited a group of civilian experts, many of whom became RNVR officers for the duration of the war.

Their first real success came when a German naval codebook was provided by the Russians, who had captured it from the cruiser *Magdeburg*. A later break came with officers finding copies of German diplomatic cyphers in the luggage of a German agent in Persia, seized when British troops captured his consulate.

German radio messages were intercepted as were their diplomatic telegrams, which had to be routed through cables that crossed British territory and both were also regularly broken.

The code-breakers were helped by German formality in composing messages, usually beginning and ending with a few easily identified set phrases. It soon became obvious, for example, that Zeppelin raids were in the offing when operational orders began with instructions not to carry certain codebooks. Movements of German ships were tracked by monitoring their call signs so that the Admiralty generally knew when major operations were being proposed and the Grand alerted. When the enemy changed a cypher it became a matter of honour among the duty code-breakers to crack the change before the end of their shift, and they usually succeeded.

Room 40's greatest triumph came in 1917 when it broke a telegram between the German Foreign Office and Zimmermann, Ambassador in Mexico, trying to entice Mexico into war against the USA by offering them Arizona, New Mexico and Texas when Germany won. Japan was also to be tempted to switch sides in return for gains in the Pacific. Having disguised the way they obtained the telegram it was released to American officials, leading to her entry into the war.

Files on Room 40 are spread between the ADM and HW series and include:

- ADM 1/23899 – Lecture by Sir James Ewing on the work of Room 40 in the First World War: text received from Lady Ewing
- ADM 223/767 – Room 40 OB war diary and logbook M05E
- ADM 223/773 – Memo on 'Political' Branch of Room 40
- HW 3/1 – Documents relating to Naval Section: covering signals intelligence and associated administration from early days of Room 40, Old Admiralty Building, to Government Code and Cypher School (GCCS)
- HW 3/35 – Founding of GCCS: applications by Room 40 staff to work in organisation, competing bids by Admiralty and War Office for senior posts.

The Intelligence Corps

Lord Esher's review of Boer War intelligence recommended the peacetime creation of a corps of intelligence gatherers which could be rapidly expanded in wartime. A list of candidates was drawn up in the War Office. On the outbreak of war they were sent to France with the British Expeditionary Force (BEF).

Anthony Clayton's book *Forearmed – A History of the Intelligence Corps* lists the officers who went to France in August 1914, along with some details of their subsequent careers. The 'other ranks' sent out to France in August were mainly grooms and officers' servants, along with a group of Special Branch officers on secondment to the Army.

By December 1917 the Intelligence Corps in France consisted of 1,225 all ranks, including 12 Women's Auxiliary Army Corps. There were 98 officers and 124 other ranks at BEF Headquarters, with a company of 9 officers and 36 other ranks attached to each Army Headquarters, a Line of Communications Company of 26 officers and 222 other ranks and other sections serving with each Corps Headquarters and various RFC squadrons.

Intelligence Corps duties
Security

One of the first duties of the Corps was security (hence the inclusion of Special Branch policemen), but it was only after a conference with the French in early 1915 that a control system was established This introduced permits to cross the Channel and divided the territory in rear of the BEF into security zones. Intelligence Corps men stationed at the ports and throughout the BEF zone monitored movements of individuals. Officers posted to most towns ran informants who reported on suspicious individuals and on sources of rumours, brothels and prostitutes, morale of the troops and black-market activities. They worked closely with French detectives.

Wireless
Special Royal Engineers units intercepted German wireless transmissions but Intelligence Corps officers decoded the intercepts and collated the information. From early 1917 most Army Corps had two interception units. A dozen Women's Auxiliary Army Corps members worked at GHQ deciphering radio messages.

Censorship
Though soldiers' letters were censored by their own officers, Intelligence Corps officers at Le Havre and other ports scanned mail for security lapses and also checked civilian mail for useful intelligence.

Photograph interpretation
By the end of 1916 every RFC reconnaissance squadron had a Corps officer, two draughtsmen and a clerk attached. Other officers worked at RFC Wing Headquarters and at RFC Headquarters interpreting photographs and collating information.

War trade
A small section of the Corps examined salvaged enemy equipment for evidence of manufacture outside Germany. Their reports went to the War Trade Intelligence Committee in London so pressure could be put on neutral manufacturers not to export to Germany.

Interrogation
Interrogation of prisoners and interviewing of civilians and released British prisoners was an important source of low-level information. Prisoners were questioned as soon after capture as possible but, occasionally, fluent German speakers were placed in camps disguised as prisoners, in order to obtain further information.

Secret service and agent running
Intelligence Corps agent runners and secret-service officers were controlled from BEF GHQ by Intelligence Section 1 (b). In early 1917 it was

commanded by Reggie Drake, who had previously been Kell's number two at MI5. His history of the organisation is in WO 106/45 – 'History of Intelligence and Secret Service Organisations'. This describes the management of GHQ intelligence in Belgium and northern France through two organisations, one at Folkestone under Major A C Cameron, the other in London under Major B A Wallinger. There was also a branch office in Paris under Captain the Honourable G J G Bruce who recruited agents among Belgians and Frenchmen in unoccupied France. Both organisations operated through Holland and maintained their own system of head men, couriers, passeurs and agents.

The two organisations were eventually placed under the control of the military attaché in The Hague and his coordinating hand soon ironed out many of the problems that having two separate networks had caused. His trained mind soon spotted agents who were working for both and being paid twice for the same information.

The secret-service networks were devoted to train watching for tracing the movements of enemy units, which was vital in drawing up the German order of battle. By counting the number of trucks and carriages it was usually quite simple to work out what kind of troops were being moved and how many there were. Watching strategic junctions and stations meant movements could be tracked efficiently. Some tasks were allotted to special agents, such as reporting on defences, shipping movements from Zeebrugge and Ostend, technical details on artillery, aviation and aerodromes and the acquisition by theft or purchase of German military documents.

Second in command of the Folkestone operation was an Intelligence Corps officer, Sigismund Payne Best, and other Corps officers were involved either in running the organisations or in interpreting their information. Among these were Captain Edward Lane Philip, Lieutenant W L McEwen and Captain Stanley Herbert Cunliffe Woolrych. Captain the Honourable G Bruce, who ran the Paris Office, managed to establish a highly successful train-watching operation in Luxembourg in 1918, sending a key agent in using a free balloon. On occasion officers would be dropped into enemy territory to gather information personally, though no list of them seems to have survived.

Corps officers also sent homing pigeons to the inhabitants of occupied territory, carried by free balloon and dropped by a clockwork mechanism after a specified time. By this method 40 per cent of messages were returned and the information was generally good, fresh and rapidly transmitted. The balloons were usually launched at about 11 pm and many replies were received at 5 am the following morning.

GHQ secret service employed about 6,000 agents in France and Belgium during the war. Of these, 98 were killed and about 600 arrested, sentenced and imprisoned.

Drake commented on his agents:

With few exceptions, all these persons have worked from motives of the highest patriotism. Considering the dangers they ran and the value of the information they provided, the cost of the service was surprisingly low. . . . Every class of person was employed, from abbes, high officials of the Gendarmerie, a Marchioness of some 60 years of age, big industrialists and prominent barristers, down to seamstresses, poachers, smugglers, bargemen and railway officials.

Among files of interest are:
• WO 106/6189 – History of the British Secret Service in Holland, 1914–1917 by Lieutenant M R K Burge gives a lot of detail on the operations run out of Holland into Belgium;
• WO 106/6192 details the honours and awards to named French, Belgian and Dutch secret-service agents;
• WO 106/6392 and WO 106/6393 contain notes and instructions on the use of carrier pigeons in France.

Identifying Intelligence Corps officers and men

There is no surviving list of Intelligence Corps officers or their men. The *Army List* is of little use for officers as they generally wore the cap badge of their original regiment or, if they were recruited specially, the General List badge. Records for officers should be in either WO 339 or WO 374 series.

The most comprehensive list of Intelligence Corps officers and men is likely to be derivable from the medal card index, which recorded the service of all men and women in the Army who were entitled to medals. Care must be taken as some Intelligence Corps officers never served abroad so did not receive medals. Many of the men who volunteered or were co-opted into the Intelligence Corps in 1914 and later wore badges of the 10th Battalion Royal Fusiliers (B) (to distinguish it from the ordinary 10th Battalion, which was a service battalion) and their medal card may only show them with that regiment – this is certainly the case with Herbert Dale Long.

Service records of Intelligence Corps other ranks should be held in TNA's WO 363 and WO 364 series, though in practice I have been unable to find any that I have looked for. Do not let this put you off, however, as 60 per

A.G.&.F. 9/~5/5796.

Room *011*.
War Office,
London, S.W.

6/8/1920.

1. Rank and Name. — *1st (a/Capt.) John Penmorlan Maine*

2. Corps. — *6th Bn: Notts & Derby Regt.*

3. Corps with which last served in. — *Intelligence Corps.*

4. Address to which orders can readily reach you. — *British Passport Control Office 44 Whitehall St. New York City USA.*

5. Date of leaving Unit or appointment. — *Oct: 13th 1919.*

6. Date of Embarkation. — *Oct 13th 1919.*

7. Port of Embarkation. — *Boulogne.*

8. Port of Disembarkation, (England). — *Folkestone.*

9. Date of Arrival in England. — *Oct 13th 1919.*

10. Name of Ship. — —

11. Cause of Return. — *Demobilisation ordered:*

12. Dates if on leave.

   From............................

   To............................

13. Authority.

14. Whether examined by a Medical Board since return from Continent. — *No.*

   (Signature)

   (Date). *23/8/20.*

   J.P. Maine. Capt.

Captain J P Maine of the Intelligence Corps' posting to SIS (in the form of the New York Passport Control Office) in 1920 is confirmed by his forwarding address when he proceeds to England from France for demobilisation.

cent of soldiers' records from the First World War were destroyed in the blitz so the finding of any record is likely to involve luck – perhaps I have just not been lucky when seeking Intelligence Corps men!

Service records for the WAAC members who worked in GHQ Radio Section are in WO 398 series, which can be downloaded via TNA's website.

A branch of the Intelligence Corps was established in Egypt in 1916 employing 'gentlemen of high standing and local experience of intelligence work' and there is a list of these in WO 32/10778. WO 32/10777 gives similar details for the Intelligence Corps that served with the Army in Salonica.

A volunteer at the current Intelligence Corps Museum is compiling a database of First World War Intelligence Corps men, so it is worth contacting them initially to see if they have details of your man.

Lieutenant Simon Magnus Castello (WO 339/64827)

Private Castello (1st Battalion, Honourable Artillery Company) was a stockbroker when he enlisted in October 1914. In April 1916 Major Howick wrote:

> Since the beginning of October he has done all the clerical and office work for the GSO 3 for the 3rd Division and he has a thoroughly good knowledge of the formations of the German army. He speaks both German and French well, having been educated in Germany. He has also worked for the Intelligence Branch of the V Corps at times of pressure.

He was promoted to 2nd Lieutenant (Special List) as Intelligence Corps Agent 4th Class and posted to HQ Intelligence Corps, GHQ. He was an Intelligence Officer at VI Corps, then a Wireless Intelligence Officer (WIO) with 5th Army HQ in April 1918, followed by a posting as WIO at 4th Army. A note dated 4 October 1918 is addressed to 'Captain Castello S M, Wireless Secn, 4th AHQ'. He was mentioned in Douglas Haig's despatch of 7 November 1917 (fourth supplement) and awarded the Military Cross on 3 June 1918. He relinquished his commission on 28 January 1919.

Lieutenant Hugh Morton Craig – Intelligence officer in Salonica and South Russia

Lieutenant Craig's file (WO 339/33888) contains one of the most detailed lists of postings that you are likely to find in any officer's file. Born in 1889, he served as a Private in the 2nd Royal Scots Fusiliers before volunteering for a commission in 1915. He had previously been a manager in the Turkish

Department of British American Tobacco. He was commissioned a Temporary Lieutenant on 11 January 1916 and eleven days later disembarked at Alexandria as an Intelligence Officer. In February he was posted to Salonica serving with 7th Mounted Brigade and the Sherwood Rangers until he was transferred to GHQ Salonica. He spent some time with the Allied Control Commission in Athens between January and May 1917 when he joined the HQs of 26 and 28 Divisions. He moved around the Salonica front and Aegean during 1917 and 1918 and on 9 November 1918 was awarded the Order of the Redeemer (Chevalier 5th Class) by the Greek King. During 1919 he was in South Russia as Temporary Captain and 1st Class Agent in the Intelligence Corps. He was at Ekaterinodar in March 1919, in Taganro in August and in Novorossisk in October. On 31 October he was transferred to the British Military Mission in South Russia from which he was gazetted out of the Army on 25 June 1920.

Given the pretty exact dates that his record provides for his postings it ought to be possible to find out more about the conditions he worked in and the units he worked with. There are War Diaries for the Salonica front in the WO 95 series at TNA, including WO 95/4793 – '7 Mounted Brigade: 1/1 Nottinghamshire and Sherwood Rangers Yeomanry' and WO 95/4793 – '7 Mounted Brigade: Headquarters'.

There are several reports from the Military Mission to South Russia in the WO 32, WO 33 and WO 106 series, including WO 32/5712, WO 33/971 and WO 106/6374. There is other material in some of the WO 158 and WO 279 series. Given the political situation in South Russia there are likely to be further reports on the situation in the FO 371 series, which are not indexed online.

Army wireless intelligence

The Army wireless and code-breaking section was MI1 (b), which grew out of a small section of MO 5 formed in 1914. By the end of the war it had 34 officers, 11 civilians and 40 female staff. Files relating to its activities are in the HW series – HW 3/184 contains 'Correspondence of MI 1b Room 40 and the Chief Censor, War Office 1916–1918 concerning diplomatic and agent activity'; HW 3/185 contains papers on codes for Russia and HW 3/186 correspondence to and from the Foreign Office 1917–1919. HW 7/35 contains an anonymous history of the section.

Chapter 7

MI5 BETWEEN THE WARS

There were rapid cuts in the intelligence budgets following the First World War and MI5 shrank to 130 staff in 1920 (KV 4/127). With Special Branch responsible for communist subversion, MI5 handled espionage and subversion within the armed forces. There were foreign spies for them to worry about – Japan made a concerted effort to obtain technical aviation information and the files on Frederick Joseph Rutland (KV 2/328 – KV 2/339) shed fascinating light on MI5's methods. Rutland was a First World War hero and RAF Officer on HMS *Eagle* with specialist knowledge of aircraft carriers when, in December 1922, GC&CS decoded a message revealing he was negotiating to enter Japanese service. MI5 monitored him but could not act due to the delicacy of its source material. Rutland retired from the RAF in 1923 and in 1924 moved to France, where SIS Paris station observed him meeting various Japanese officials. He left for Japan in July 1924 where he was watched by SIS and the naval attaché.

In 1928 Rutland returned home and MI5's file became dormant, but in March 1933 GC&CS again intercepted coded Japanese messages referring to FURUYAMA codename for a former British officer negotiating with them for 'collecting war time information'. MI5 gradually worked out that he had been a naval officer, spoke some Japanese and had been in Japan and began investigating former RN officers matching these criteria. Further messages revealed that FURUYAMA had been renamed SHINKAWA and in July intercepted messages that revealed that he had booked passage to the USA and Japan using Thomas Cook. Investigations at Cooks showed that SHINKAWA was Rutland. Round the clock mail interception and shadowing followed.

The delicacy of the source material (radio intercepts and broken codes) meant no action could be taken against Rutland but his activities in the USA were monitored by SIS and he was routinely followed when he returned to Britain. Eventually, in 1941, with the FBI hot on his trail, he returned to Britain and was interned. Though he and his friends repeatedly proclaimed his innocence they could not, of course, be shown MI5's proof, and for many years after Rutland's suicide at the end of the war it was thought to be a terrible mistake.

There were many other investigations – suspected German agents continued to be monitored and a complex series of investigations into the Federated Press of America, its founder William Ewer and associates eventually revealed a Soviet espionage ring that had two agents within Special Branch. They were exposed and forced to resign. Ewer's organisation had also spied on MI5 and SIS, having simply followed Kell from his home to MI5 and SIS offices, then tried to make contact with their staff. The file of Arthur Francis Lakey (KV 2 989 and KV 2/990), a former policeman who worked for FPA, reveals that they had managed to contact a Mrs Moon who worked for SIS in their Melbury Road office and, by pretending to be American secret-service officers, had persuaded her to give them information about her work. Mrs Moon had, subsequently, told SIS, who called in MI5. Unable to substantiate her story, they had her dismissed. The FPA also uncovered an SIS office in Adam Street run by a man named Crowley who lived in Tufnell Park.

In 1931 MI5 took over the Special Branch secret-service branch SS1 and Maxwell Knight's agents, with an increased mandate to examine sedition and communism generally. In 1934 this expanded to cover fascism. The Security Service now came under the authority of the Home Secretary.

In 1937 plans were drafted for expansion in time of war and a gradual enlargement was begun. It was not to prove sufficient.

MI5 files

- KV 2 series: this series consists mainly of files on individuals (though some organisations are included). Individuals featured include many famous subjects such as Lenin, Trotsky, Rudolf Hess and Compton-Mackenzie (tried under the Official Secrets Act in 1932 for a writing a book on the secret service in Greece), but also scores of spies, couriers, suspect communists and fascists and persons who had come to MI5's attention. These files contain most references to individuals and will be the ones of most interest to family historians.

- KV 3 series: the Subject Files deal with matters such as foreign secret services, communist activities, fascist organisations and enemy propaganda. There are frequent references to individuals but you have to dig to find them.
- KV 4 series: the Policy Files, which include the Section Histories for the Second World War. These are invaluable if you know which section a relative worked in.
- KV 5 series: the Organisation Files which examine organisations (but not secret services) that came to the MI5's attention. These include pacifist, Jewish, left-wing and pro-German groups and frequently name their members so can be fruitful for research if an ancestor belonged to one of these organisations.
- KV 6 series: the List Files were compiled during the course of specific investigations into, for example, compromised SOE networks. Some concern specific individuals.

Reading a KV 2 (personal) file

Only a tiny proportion of MI5's personal files have been released. By the late 1940s there were over 600,000. The file on Christian LINDEMANS, alias Christian BRANT (KV 2/231 – KV 2/237) is PF 600,513 and was probably created in 1944.

To March 2008 a total of 2,829 KV 2 files have been released, many of these having several files covering one individual. Many personal files were legitimately destroyed once investigations were over and there is evidence of this in surviving files when a mark is made against a cross-reference to a destroyed file.

There are common features and things to look out for:

Each file has, in the front, an index to the papers inside. Very often large parts of the index will have been scored lightly through, indicating that the papers have been destroyed. This was part of the normal weeding process whereby papers without ongoing relevance were destroyed to save space. It is always worth checking the index for references that might relate to your interest even if MI5 felt they were not worth keeping. Also, as you go through the file, you are likely to come across documents that have been wholly, or partly, redacted. Though MI5's current weeders seem to have caught on to this, in earlier releases they frequently did not redact the index, so some information about the document can be found. There are frequently internal MI5 minutes in the index which do not appear in the file itself.

Check the original file number, but take care – the file for former SIS agent Sidney Reilly (KV 2/827) has a cover number of PF 864,103, which implies a very late creation, but refers to itself internally as PF 25,096 which is more in keeping with a file created during the First World War. You can also check whether the original file was a PP, PFR or other sequence file.

The material in PF series files is miscellaneous to say the least. Frequently there will be copies of GPO intercepted correspondence, cross-references from other files, messages from other intelligence agencies (SIS, MI1c, IPI, Special Branch), interviews with sources (sometimes secret agents, but often people associated with the subject who do not even realise that it is MI5 they are talking to), details of travel abroad provided by Special Branch or Passport Control Office, intercepted telephone messages and, in some of the later files, what appear to be recordings taken from 'bugs'. I have even seen photographs of penguins at London Zoo!

Personal files start at the back of the first file in the sequence so the first document that brought the subject to MI5's attention will be here. Quite often this is just a mention from a file relating to someone else, which would have been noted on a card in Registry. When MI5 decided that someone merited a file of their own all these references would be collated and copied to the new file. These cross-references can be important as they give a broader picture of the individual's contacts, and they can also refer to files that have not yet been released, or have been destroyed. We know that MI5 had a file on the black magician Aleister Crowley from such a cross-reference, even though his file is not released. Cross-references are usually indicated by square brackets around the name as it stands in the text and a handwritten file number, for example:

PF 39747 HOPKINS
[Roy Cecil Hopkins] – British – Flat A 37, Queensborough Terrace, Hyde Park, Journalist

Even if the file has been destroyed, or has not been released, you can at least know that the subject had come sufficiently to MI5's attention to make them create a file. There is nothing to prevent you from contacting MI5 to see if the file can be made available. This has worked for some researchers, though I understand that it is a long process as the file has to be located and reviewed before any possible release.

People mentioned in the file who do not have their own files were 'carded', i.e. their details were placed in the Registry's extensive card index so that they could be cross-referenced in future. Periodically the card index was reviewed and names removed and a stamp 'DECARDED' and a date will tell you when MI5 lost interest in that individual.

It is also worth looking for inserts into an original MI5 file from Scotland Yard's files following the merger with Guy Liddell's SS1 department in 1931. These can generally be noted by SZ , SY or Y stamps on the papers. Many files also contain copies of burnt documents from earlier files that were damaged when a German bomb hit the Registry during the time it was stored at Wormwood Scrubs in 1940.

The PF files were designed to hold all the papers relating to the suspect individual, but there are occasions when it is obvious that things are missing.

Released in March 2008 was KV 2/2821, the file on Hungarian astrologer Louis De Wohl, who worked for SOE and the Political Warfare Executive as an adviser on propaganda. There is no mention on the file that De Wohl also worked for Naval Intelligence's Admiral Godfrey, even though MI5 were certainly aware of this. Guy Liddell, head of B Branch, recorded in his diary in early 1941: 'DNI is employing Louis de Wohl to read the horoscopes of the most important Admirals in the Navy, and those of Hitler, Mussolini, Darlan and Portal. . . . It is believed that DNI himself is a strong believer in astrology. . . . The whole business seems to me to be highly misleading and dangerous.' There is no mention of this connection to NID in De Wohl's KV 2 file.

On 20 May 1940 MI5's chief agent runner, Maxwell Knight, led a search party to the flat of Tyler Kent, a cypher clerk at the American Embassy, and 'discovered' a hoard of secret telegrams. This led to Kent's arrest and imprisonment. The building that housed the flat was large and complex but, as American Diplomat Franklin Gowen noticed, Knight led the search party directly to the flat without asking the maid for directions. It was plain to Gowen that Knight had visited the flat previously, but there is absolutely no reference to this in Kent's files (KV 2/543 – 545).

The file on Leonid Krassin, Soviet diplomat and leading participant in the Russo-British trade talks in the early 1920, contains a brief mention: 'a year ago we opened Krassin's safe deposit box at Selfridge's'. It goes on to list the contents of the box. The operation seems to have been a Scotland Yard rather than an MI5 one, but there are no other references to this on the file. Whether it was done with a warrant, by having a quiet chat with Selfridge's security manager or by clandestine means, one would suspect that there should be some mention of it.

It is rare on any of the KV 2 files to find any real reference to the actual investigations that took place, though presumably notes were made and meetings held in their course. Much has to be deduced from the file contents and from cross-referencing and analysing their contents.

MI5 file references

Even without an actual PF file it is sometimes possible to deduce something about the individual from their file reference.

Most personal files are headed PF and, in general, files were created sequentially so the lower the file number the earlier it was created. In the very early days the files were arranged alphabetically but this was changed to a numerical system late in 1914 or early 1915.

The file on German spy Vieyra is PF 5831 and for George Vaux Bacon, an American who spied for Germany, is PF 10199. The file on Mata Hari is even lower at PF 2917.

In addition to normal PF files MI5 created a series of sub-sections in their Registry holding specialist personal files. First of these were the Peace Propaganda series (PP) created early in the First World War when MI5 began looking at groups and individuals campaigning against the war including pacifists, left-wing socialists and groups opposed to conscription.

Another series of distinct personal files is the PFR series, where R stands for Russian. These were started in early 1919 when MI5's Mr Farina began compiling a Russian Black List. He created the files by cross-referencing mentions of Russians in previous correspondence and compiled most of the early files retrospectively. It is likely that the first 3,000 or so PFR were created in 1919 so a number lower than that is likely to show an MI5 interest from this period.

Not all PFR files refer to Russians. Arthur Ransome, British journalist in Russia during the First World War (and an SIS agent), has a reference PFR 301; the Reverend Hewlett Johnson, known as the 'Red Dean', had certainly never been to Russia when his file was set up, probably in 1921. He was, however, connected to the 'Hands off Russia' campaign.

There were at least three other runs of PF files, though not enough have been released to allow for serious analysis. PFNE files covered suspects in the Near East; PFFE those in the Far East; and PFI dealt with Indians. There was also a run of files on Irish suspects. Once again, it is likely that British subjects living in, or connected with, the geographical area might have one of these files.

Strange bedfellows

The early 1920s saw the rise of a number of private intelligence organisations for spying on trade unions, the Communist Party, Labour Party and sources of industrial unrest. Though most were little more than the curious fantasies of right-leaning individuals the more serious of them maintained contacts with the official intelligence services and the authorities generally.

Connections with these shadowy private bodies began during the First World War when MI5 was in close touch with the Anti-German Union, receiving reports from them about attempts to disrupt anti-war meetings and demonstrations. The Anti-German Union was founded by Sir George Makgill, who was cousin of MI5's Maldwyn Makgill Haldane, head of MI5 H – Makgill's mother and Haldane's father were brother and sister. Makgill was, apparently, introduced to SIS Head of Production Desmond Morton by

Carrying the whole world of MI5 on his shoulders, Major Maldwyn Makgill Haldane, in charge of H Section. H Section's work in carding suspects, creating files and running the massive Registry was the key to MI5's success. (from the MI5 cartoon book *Secrets of Waterloo(se) House*)

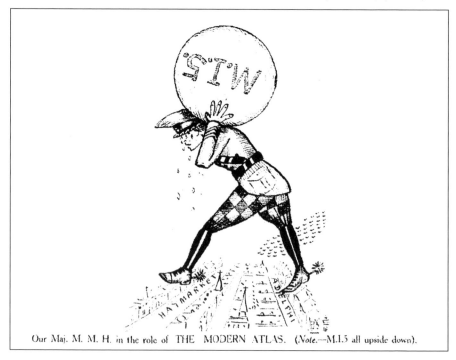

Our Maj. M. M. H. in the role of THE MODERN ATLAS. (*Note.*—M.I.5 all upside down).

Vernon Kell in 1920 or 1921. Makgill (now head of the British Empire Union) established a private Industrial Intelligence Bureau financed by the Federation of British Industries and the Coal Owners and Ship Owners Associations. His agents provided material to Morton on Soviet and other organisations in Britain and Makgill's son Donald also worked for the organisation. He later worked briefly for SOE and his Personnel File HS 9/978/1, though much redacted when it talks about this early work, describes his father's profession as 'Intelligence (Industry-Politic)'. There is also a faint pencil note the weeders may have missed that says 'Experience of Intelligence work with Police 1922–1926'. George MakGill died in 1926 and his secret organisation seems to have faded away with him, though one of his protégés, C H Maxwell Knight, continued to run his own organisation.

Knight belonged to another (and to modern eyes) more sordid group, the early fascists, which had sprung up in Britain following Mussolini's rise in Italy. Described by a much more odious and dyed in the wool fascist, Arnold Leese, as not real fascists, just 'Conservatives with knobs on', the first were the British Fascisti. This group was organised along paramilitary lines and boasted an 'intelligence and counterespionage' department that claimed to operate secret cells in the trade unions and Communist Party. Like all of these fringe groups, the British Fascisti splintered with the main body becoming the British Fascists.

The British fascists did have one important intelligence asset and this was Maxwell Knight. KV 3/57 – 'Activities of the British Fascist Organisation in the UK (excluding the British Union of Fascists)' – contains several copies of a detailed report on the fascists, including details of their intelligence organisation. At some point in the past this document has been carefully redacted (not, apparently, at the time of release to TNA) but not carefully enough. On one copy, when discussing the intelligence organisation, the name Knight, which has been carefully removed from the other copies, remains clearly visible.

Further proof comes from a Foreign Office file (FO 3271/11384). A report submitted to the Foreign Office by J F C Carter of Special Branch in September 1926 detailed a conversation with two senior fascists regarding attempts to set up branch for British expatriates in Italy. Carter cautioned against the dangers of such an enterprise and the fascists agreed to suspend their activities, giving Carter a list of their newly formed Council. At the bottom of the list is Maxwell Knight Esq.

Knight ran a small number of agents carefully placed within communist and left-wing organisations. He had known MakGill and it may have been MakGill that introduced him to Desmond Morton of SIS. In the late 1920s he supplied Morton with information. He was also known to Colonel Carter of Special Branch. In 1931, following complaints about SIS effectively running agents (i.e. Knight's people) inside Britain the organisation became officially part of MI5 and Knight an MI5 officer (though he first appears on the MI5 Staff List in May 1936). His agents continued as an MI5 resource.

Finding MI5 staff

There are various MI5 staff lists covering the inter-war period in KV 4/127. As well as a general chart showing the responsibilities of officers over the period there are more detailed lists for May 1920, September 1937 and September 1938. Many staff stayed with the Service for many years. There are some organisational charts and explanations of each section's work so you can understand what they were doing and, hopefully, find other files providing more information.

MI5 agents

Between the wars MI5 ran only a handful of agents. A list of expenses for 1921–1922 (KV 4/198) shows only five agents, known as J, H, C, JW and US being paid £1,586 8s between them, with a separate sum of £180 listed for 'B agents'. Who these agents are is hard to say, though JW may be the Winkelmann recorded as an agent in the KV 1 files. Maxwell Knight recorded that before the Second World War, with the exception of his M section, MI5 ran less than a dozen agents, one of whom was Klop Ustinov, father of actor Peter Ustinov, a German journalist, codenamed U35.

Wide reading around the subject can often assist in identifying an agent. There are repeated references in MI5 files to a Scotland Yard agent known only as VSO. He is obviously Russian, with connections to the Russian Trade Mission in London. Documents in the Russian archives in Nigel West's *The Crown Jewels – The British Secrets Exposed by the KGB Archives* mention that former Russian Consul Victor Sablin was known by the Russians to be watching them, using various of his friends as sub-agents. Could VSO be Victor Sabline? He had an MI5 file (PFR 417), the low number of which suggests that it was created very early.

Maxwell Knight's agents are identifiable because their agent numbers are prefixed with an M. Occasional personal details on them appear in the files so identification may be possible. Agent M/7 was close to Denis Nowell

Pritt, King's Counsel and Labour MP for North Hammersmith (identified by Soviet defector Walter Krivitsky as 'one of the chief recruiting agents for Soviet underground organisations in the United Kingdom'). Pritt proposed M/7 for membership of the Haldane Club. Records for the Haldane no longer exist, but it could be a vital clue for someone seeking that particular agent.

The Special Branch Secret Departments – SS1 and SS2

In addition to Special Branch's work in acting as MI5's arresting officers, investigating Irish and anarchist terrorism, illegal drugs, checking the credentials of foreigners and acting as VIP bodyguards, the Branch ran two small secret-service sections, SS1 and SS2, which were formed in 1919.

SS2 collated information on suspects at home. It had only three staff – Miss McCulloch and Miss Saunders ran the Registry, assisted by a clerk. It dealt with British subjects engaged in revolutionary and seditious activities, liaising with chief constables in Britain and monitoring their activities abroad through liaison with SS1. Scotland Yard paid £2,000 pa to county and borough police forces to subsidise local investigations.

SS1, consisting of Captains Miller and Liddell and two clerks, was liaison section with SIS (in effect the Home Section of SIS). It ran agents and informers within revolutionary organisations; collated information on revolutionary movements and individuals abroad or working in embassies in London; examined passport applications of suspicious foreigners (including all Russian applicants); advised the Home Office on the exclusion of undesirable aliens; liaised with police in the Dominions, the Colonies (through the Colonial Office); liaised with foreign governments hostile to revolutionary movements; checked foreign revolutionary films and literature for the Home Office and Censor; watched the arms trade at home and abroad; and assisted SIS in the tracing of forged bank notes.

In 1931 personality clashes between Liddell, Miller and Lieutenant Colonel Carter, Head of Special Branch (and former head of MI5g in the First World War) and a growing suspicion within the Branch that SS1 was really just an SIS outpost led to discussions about the section's future. These are detailed in FO 1093/74. Since the early 1920s SS1 had built up considerable expertise and, after initial discussions around their joining SIS, they were placed under Colonel Kell at MI5. SS2 remained at Scotland Yard but SS1's files, as well as Liddell and Miller, were transferred to MI5 on 15 October 1931 and their files were amalgamated.

SS1 files and records

Most surviving SS1 material is in the MI5 PF files, but can still be recognised. Between 1919 and 1926 SS1 received their information from SIS via its section 1b so that any CX marked as coming from that section can be spotted as originally being intended for SS1. After the establishment of SIS Section V material passed to SS1 from this source, so any CX marked as Section V sourced, unless marked as being copied to MI5, can be reckoned as SS1 material. From 1931 onwards all material to MI5 (some of which, relating to the armed forces or espionage, had been forwarded via MI1c) was sourced from Section V.

SS1 material can also be spotted in the MI5 PF files if addressed to Captain Miller or Captain Liddell before October 1931. Other material is frequently stamped SY, SZ or Y. SY is, I believe, a normal Special Branch stamp and SZ the SS1 specific stamp.

As one of SS1's principal customers was the Home Office, material frequently turns up in HO series, particularly that dealing with communism and extremism. HO 144/6682 ('DISTURBANCES: Communist Party: activities') consists of an informant's report obtained by the Home Office itself, dealing with Soviet funding in Australia and Britain. Captain Liddell was impressed with the information, suspecting that the informant had previously been in touch with SS1, and asked urgently for details so that he could resume contact. Other reports occasionally turn up in the FO 371 series where they relate to foreign revolutionaries.

There is an interesting report in CAB 127/366 ('Report on function and duties of Special Branch, SS1 and SS2') which sets out the responsibilities of SS1, SS2 and Special Branch itself.

CAB 127/364 contains comments from SIS on the overlapping responsibilities of MI6, MI5, Scotland Yard, IPI, GC&CS and passport-control department and the problems caused by their not being integrated.

Chapter 8

SIS BETWEEN THE WARS

In 1919 SIS formally adopted the military control officers who, as passport-control officers, became SIS station heads in their respective countries. Under cover of issuing travel documents SIS representatives were able to keep in contact with agents travelling abroad. Though in theory not supposed to carry out spying in the country they were based in (the so called third-party rule), this was not always honoured. There are documents discussing SIS's budget in the early years in KV 4/151 and it is clear that Cumming had to argue hard to maintain his organisation as a worldwide one, stressing 'the situations all over the world are so complex that greater vigilance on the part of SIS is required than in 1914'.

With Cumming's death in 1923 his position was passed to the Director of Naval Intelligence, Sir Hugh Sinclair, a privately wealthy man who, it is strongly suspected, used much of his wealth to subsidise the service.

SIS managed to maintain most of their passport-control offices throughout the world but they were not the only means of collecting information. The Trade Mission in Moscow, which was established in 1921, and presumably one of the 'schemes for obtaining information from Moscow' (KV 4/151) contained a number of SIS officers. SIS had excellent sources at all levels of the Russian state, including a member of the Politburo, and received regular copies of minutes of their meetings, as well as from the Russian Foreign Office. They had an extensive knowledge of the organisation of the Russian secret services and provided the Foreign Office with a structure chart of their organisation (FO 371/9337). The Comintern, the international organisation of Communist Parties, was seriously penetrated and their operations frequently compromised. Though often accused of having few sources of their own inside Russia, and relying on seriously penetrated White Russian organisations for information, it is clear that SIS was quite well aware that the Whites were penetrated by the Russian secret services and had good sources quite independent of them. Gas warfare was a major target and much information was collected from Russia, but also from many other countries.

SIS Liaison sections collected lists of questions from other government departments and passed them to Production (headed by Desmond Morton), who forwarded them to agents in the field. When answers were received they were passed back to the department via the Liaison sections. There is a diagram of SIS organisational structure, *c*. 1923 in Appendix 7. In 1925 a new circulating section, section V, was established to liaise with Special Branch and IPI about subversion and this later (1931) assumed liaison duties with MI5 which had previously been handled through MI1c at the War Office.

During the 1930s the revival of Hitler's Germany meant many of SIS's priorities switched to this target (though Germany's clandestine relations with Russia had always been under investigation). The passport-control offices in Eastern Europe now found themselves looking in both directions – East to Russia and West to Germany. Their cover was now threadbare – the Germans were trying to infiltrate the PCO in The Hague and Russian defector Walter Krivitsky revealed in his 1940 interrogation that the Russians had also worked out the SIS connection.

Finding SIS officers and agents

SIS relied heavily on contacts it had built up during the First World War. Many of the PCOs were formerly in the Intelligence Corps – Maurice Jeffes, PCO in New York in the early 1920s, Paris in the early 1930s and later head of the Passport Office had been in the Corps, as had John Maine his deputy and successor in New York, and Forbes-Dennis and Sington who were PCOs in Austria in the 1920s. Many of the former RNVR officers also continued to serve – Lieutenant Commander Ernest Boyce was PCO in Finland until he was (supposedly) retired in 1927, and Wilfred Dunderdale remained with SIS until after the Second World War. Agents too were recruited from this select band – John Henry Leather and his two associates arrested for spying in Paris in 1925 were former Intelligence Corps men.

If you suspect that a relative was in SIS between the wars and they were old enough to have served during the First World War then it really is worth checking back for clues in their service record. A few serving Army officers were attached to SIS and they can usually be found in the *Army List* 'serving under Foreign Office'. The June 1930 *Army List* records five officers employed under the Foreign Office: Major D J F Morton (Desmond Morton) was Head of Production for SIS and Captains Giffey, Shelley and Kensington and Lieutenant Nicholson were all serving with SIS, three as PCOs.

It is worth looking for references to individuals in the Foreign Office indexes, though after about 1924 references to identifiable SIS people become scarcer. A scan of the Gestapo Black List is also advisable as the suspected British agents in it do sometimes go back to the 1920s.

Passport Control

Passport Control served a genuine function of its own, as well as acting as cover for the local SIS station. Applicants for visas to travel to Britain were vetted by the local office but referred to London if there was doubt about their bona fides or the desirability of their visiting. In the larger passport-control offices (such as Paris, New York and Berlin), most of the staff were probably concerned purely with passport work.

At first all PCOs were accredited through Scotland Yard with their local police force. This process began to lapse in the late 1920s but it is clear that the passport-control officer, because of his connections with the local police, was sometimes involved as a contact point on general security matters. Frank Foley, PCO Berlin, accompanied MI5's Guy Liddell when he took part in talks with Nazi officials in 1933 (KV 4/111) after they had raided the headquarters of the German Communist Party. In 1922 the Vienna PCO, Mr Forbes-Dennis, was involved in tracking arms being smuggled out of Austria into Palestine.

Passport Control records

Records of the individual passport-control offices have generally either not survived or not been released. Records for individuals do occasionally throw up references to PCOs but these have to be searched for. A Home Office file on Trotsky's attempts to visit Britain (HO 382/7), for example, contains correspondence from Mr Elder, PCO Constantinople, in 1929 and Mr C S Collinson working in the PCO, Paris, in 1934. There are occasional notes from PCOs in KV 2 files where applications have been made by suspects to visit Britain.

The records of the Foreign Office's Chief Clerk's Department are administrative but include many documents relating to Passport Control.

Our Ref: BG/11361

BRITISH PASSPORT CONTROL OFFICE,

TIERGARTENSTRASSE 17.

BERLIN W. 10

27th April 1928.

It Berlin''
Lützow 7810.''

Abraham Ananevitch KISSIN. (Soviet).

Reference H.O. No. B.495 and my BG/11361/BG/
22276 dated 24.4.28.

The application of the above to proceed to the United Kingdom for a period of two weeks is submitted for decision.

2. The purpose of his visit is set out in paragraph 11 of the application form.

3. These application forms have been received from the Norwegian Legation through the civil post.

4. Please see also my BG/22276 dated 27.4.28.

PASSPORT CONTROL OFFICER,
GERMANY.

As part of their normal function Passport Control Offices granted visas and this is an application for a visa from the Berlin Passport Control Office to the London Passport Control Office in 1929.

Among the numerous files that may produce information are:
- FO 366/794 contains a complete list of passport-control officers, assistant passport-control officers and their staff from 1921, along with details of their salaries.
- FO 366/808 details passport-control office accounts, but does not name individuals.
- FO 366/985 includes a discussion into the legal status of PCO Mr Nicholson and mentions his predecessor Mr Farina.
- FO 366/986, though not listed as doing so in TNA's catalogue, also contains estimates of passport-control offices worldwide.

It is clear from redactions in some of the post-war FO 366 files that some PCOs continued to have SIS functions even after the Second World War.

There are also various Treasury papers that mention names; key among these is T 162/76 – 'Passport Control Office; Staff and organisation of Passport Control Offices abroad'. This names all the PCOs and most of their assistants, 1925–1926.

The Vienna PCO

Germany occupied Austria in March 1938 and on 17 August arrested the Passport Control Officer and SIS Station Chief Captain Thomas Kendrick. The two principal SIS secretaries, Betty Hodgson and Margaret Holmes, were evacuated. Holmes went on to work in the Austrian Section of SOE and her personnel file (HS 9/733/4) records:

> She was specially selected owing to her knowledge of Austria and her experience of Secret Intelligence gained during her several years work in Austria. (When, following on the Anschluss, the organisation for which she worked together with the chief persons connected with it were denounced to the Gestapo, Mrs Holmes was also implicated. Fortunately she managed to get out of Austria without being arrested, in which she was more lucky than her chief).

There is a rare insight into the staff and workings of the Vienna Passport Control Office in 1938 in FO 366/1036. Curiously neither Betty Hodgson nor Margaret Holmes are mentioned, but there is a complete list of the other staff, including Mr K C Benton, Temporary Examiner with the duties of examining applicants, correspondence and assisting the PCO; Miss M Weller, an Examiner, who examined applicants, correspondence and accounts and supervised the Lady Examiners; and Miss V Molesworth, Secretary, in charge of checking the visa-fee book and stamps, of the visa-fee cash, enciphering and dealing with correspondence. Also named are Miss Lloyd-Phillips, Miss M E Wood, Miss C R E Eady and Mrs R Howe, who are all listed as secretaries, along with Miss R Birkett, Mr F G Garrett, Mr W Steedman, Mr W F Dorrington and Miss E T Mapleston, who have various clerks duties. There were also eleven Austrian staff whose duties ranged from those of Herr Neubert, who kept the index cards and sent out notices of permits received, to Herr Seemayer, who was in charge of all the German staff and helped Mr Dorrington collect fees, to a variety of porters, telephonists and reception clerks, who also gave out forms and basic information.

Vienna Passport Control Office was, in October 1938, dealing with

200 enquiries per day from people seeking to visit, or move to, parts of the British Empire. About 100 of these enquiries per day turned into an actual application.

Laurence Collas – a British intelligence officer in Russia

During the early 1920s SIS had a group of intelligence officers working in Moscow, under cover of the British Trade Mission. One of the junior members of the Mission was Laurence Collas and the Foreign Office index cards confirmed his intelligence connections.

The index produced two references to an L Collas, leading to the same file in the Russian Consular Series for 1918, FO 369/1022. A letter from his wife gives the address: '2nd Lt L Collas, Military Control Office, "Syren", BEF North Russia' and another from the Foreign Office confirms it. The *Army List* had no references to Lieutenant Collas, but his medal card said 'Held Local Rank of 2nd Lieutenant' which explained this. KV 1/31 sets out the duties of the Murmansk Port Control Officer, including that he had been in contact with MI5 in London, but unfortunately this does not confirm he was Laurence Collas.

The index for 1919 provided more of interest. A curriculum vitae in FO 371/4009, details of members of the British Mission to the Baltic States, gives Laurence's life and service up to 1919. He was 34, privately educated on Jersey until 1897 then at Pitman's Metropolitan School, London, until 1904. In March 1914 he went to Russia as secretary to the British branch of the Westinghouse Electric and Manufacturing Co. From February 1917 to April 1918 he was secretary to the Caucasus branch of the Anglo-Russian Commission at Tiflis. From July 1918 to November 1918 he was Port Control Officer at Murmansk.

Two of his fellow Baltic Mission members were SIS officers. Transport Officer Captain Norman Dewhurst had spent two years working for SIS in Greece, and Intelligence Officer Alfred Sington is noted: 'In spite of his German parentage on one side Capt. Sington has been accepted by the War Office (MI1c) as the Intelligence representative'.

Collas went to Moscow in the summer of 1921, along with at least two other SIS officers, Oswald Rayner, who had been closely involved with the Rasputin murder, and Gerald Fitzwilliams, who had been Assistant Passport Control Officer in Vienna. A fourth member, Major Charles Dunlop, had served in Siberia from March 1920 to February 1921, attached to the Japanese HQ at Vladivistock for 'intelligence duties under the Military Attache, Tokyo'.

According to Collas' memoirs he was sent to St Petersburg with Thomas Preston, former British Consul in Ekaterinberg. This is confirmed by a mention in the Foreign Office index, though the file is not preserved.

The two men were given a huge room in the Hotel Europe, though Preston suspected the luxurious surroundings were to allow the Russians to keep them under surveillance.

We took careful notice of the exact arrangement of various articles in his bags and established beyond doubt that they were being tampered with. Then we ordered the maid not to enter our room during our absence. But this made no difference. Our cipher and code books we kept in a strong box under a Chubb lock. We never knew whether they cracked that, but actually neither that particular cipher nor the code had been regarded by our Foreign Office as secret for years and, consequently, would never be used for really secret messages.

British intelligence officer Laurence Collas in later life. Collas served in Murmansk in 1919, in the Baltic in 1919 and with the Trade Mission in Moscow and Petrograd in the early 1920s. (with grateful thanks to Rena)

Attempts were made by Russians to get them to transmit messages or articles to relatives abroad. 'These, Preston warned me, were not genuine visitors and their pathetic tales were all lies. They were spies sent by the Secret Police to catch us out in the abuse of their diplomatic privilege.'

Their precautions proved valueless, not through their carelessness but through the good nature of Mrs Collas, who was persuaded to carry some share certificates across the frontier for some friends. She was stopped, searched and the certificates found. Though Preston pulled all the right strings and exposed it as a plot, the Russians refused to back down and insisted on Collas' own expulsion. I can find no reference to this in the Foreign Office indexes, though Collas did leave Russia at this time.

Laurence and his wife moved to Queensland, Australia, where he became a photographer, and in the Second World War a Post Office censor opening letters to and from Russia.

A spy who disappeared – Sidney Hurst Tomes/Stephen Henry Turner

Sidney Tomes is mentioned in a War Diary for the 1918 Murmansk campaign as being connected with an intelligence officer of interest to me.

Foreign Office index cards produced some references, the first (FO 369/1016), dated 26 December 1917, mentions his appointment as Vice Consul at the town of Torneo. 'Commissaries of the People having objected to the activity of the British and French Military Control Officers at Torneo, it has been thought advisable to recall Lieutenant Gruner for work elsewhere.' Tornea was vital in the Military Control system as the main point through which people and goods passed from Sweden into Russia and was widely used by smugglers and spies.

A note dated 26 December 1917 says: 'Sidney Hurst Tomes (a natural born British subject) to be acting VC Tornea. He has previously worked in the Military Control Office in Petrograd.'

A note dated 27 January 1918 from acting Vice Consul Gillespie says: 'Acting Vice Consul Gruner proceeded to Petrograd 26th January leaving me in charge'. Consul Lindlay in Petrograd explained a couple of days later: 'I regret that by oversight I forgot to report that MI1c officer required Mr Tomes services elsewhere and I recommended Mr Gillespie in his place.' This confirmed that Tomes was employed by SIS under their cover name, MI1c.

On 31 August 1918 the Bolshevik Secret Police attacked the Petrograd Embassy, and the office of the Military Control nearby. Tomes' boss, Lieutenant Boyce, was arrested at the Embassy and Tomes captured in the raid on the Control Office. They were held, with other British officials, for six weeks in the Fortress of Saints Peter and Paul and were released following negotiations in return for the Bolshevik diplomat Maxim Litinov, who had been detained in London.

On 3 May 1919 Sidney Tomes wrote to the Foreign Office from his parents' home at Countesthorpe Vicarage, Leicestershire, applying for a position in the Consular Service (FO 369/1327). Quite how SIS had lost touch with Sidney since his return to Russia is not know, but on his application he wrote that he was born on 15 June 1890 and had 'been engaged as foreign representative for Messrs Faire Bros & Co Ltd, Leicester, for some 9 years and on their behalf have visited France, Germany, Holland,

Belgium, Switzerland, Denmark, Norway, Sweden and Russia'. He spoke German, French and Russian fluently and that 'my knowledge of Spanish was formerly good, but I am somewhat out of practice'. On 23 May the Foreign Office wrote to Sidney that there were currently no vacancies, but they would hold his details on file.

After this, apart from ongoing claims against the Russians for compensation for his arrest, Sidney Tomes vanishes from the Foreign Office record.

With the help of the Tomes Family History Society I was able to find details of Sidney's family and date of death. They found a nephew in South Africa who remembered receiving letters from his uncle in the 1930s. Sidney had been living in Estonia where the nephew thought he had been working as a missionary.

Sidney Tomes/Stephen Turner, early 1930s. His family were unaware of his supposed change of name. (via the Tomes Family History Association)

I then found the Card Index to British Subjects in Estonia (FO 514/6), which is arranged alphabetically, and went immediately to where Sidney Tomes' card should be. There was nothing but, having experienced muddled card indexes before, I went though all the Ts and found a card for 'Stephen Henry Turner (Tomes)' giving his father as the Reverend S H Tomes and his date of birth as 15 June 1890. It had to be the same man and with a new name the search became much easier.

In March 1922 the British Consul at Reval (now Tallin) advised the Foreign Office that:

> Mr Turner has informed me that he has received a months leave and at the end of that period he will not be resuming his duties as British Passport Officer. . . . it was his intention to enter business in Reval. . . . in partnership with a German subject, named Eggers, who has been employed in the Darlehns Kasse Ost, working in the German Legation in Reval. . . . Mr Eggers is starting an Import/Export Business.

The index card from the British Consulate in Estonia proving that Tomes and Turner were identical.

Major Spencer at the Passport Office replied unconcernedly 'Mr Turner will choose his own line in life and associates, no doubt, now that his official connections have ceased.'

A search on Eggers in the Foreign Office indexes produced a reference to an Eggers planning to use fast motor boats for trading along the coast of Estonia, but the file has not survived. I do not know if this is the same Eggers connected with Tomes/Turner, but such a business would have provided excellent cover for intelligence operations in the Gulf of Finland.

Apart from the Estonian card index Turner vanishes from the British record, but the Estonian National Archive could help. They produced a registration card dated October 1928, showing Stephen Henry Turner as a British Consular Secretary. There is no reference to this in any British records. His index card, which gives his occupation as 'Merchant', contains a note that he left Estonia on 30 September 1939 – at the time of the Soviet occupation. Presumably he returned to Britain via Finland. I can trace nothing of what he did during the war – there are no Foreign Office references to him and he does not appear in the Imperial List of Civil

Servants. His will says he lived at Fernbank, Portsmouth Road, Roehampton, London. He describes himself as a secretary and does not appear to have ever married.

He died on 3 October 1960, aged 70, in Twyford Abbey Nursing Home. Although his last definite recorded Government post was in 1922, his death certificate gives his occupation as 'Civil Servant (Retired)'.

The use of commercial cover

Not all SIS people worked abroad in passport-control offices. For operational purposes many used commercial cover. SIS's first officer in China in 1918, Mr Frodsham, was a Marconi employee, and Marconi, with huge business connections with the Government, also employed ex-SIS man Stephen Alley and Adrian Simpson, the War Office's radio expert.

British American Tobacco (BAT) crops up regularly. The range of BAT's operations gave scope for wide-ranging foreign travel. Oswald Rayner, an SIS officer who served in Russia during the First World War, worked for BAT in the 1920s and Ernest Boyce, former PCO in Helsinki (and probably still an operative SIS man), worked in the tobacco industry in the 1930s. Other SIS men with tobacco connections included Sidney Reilly and Stephen Alley. Roger Hollis, who went on to become Director General of MI5 from 1956–1965, worked for BAT in China in the late 1930s and one has to wonder if he was an SIS man at that time.

Even without involving the secret services the British Government relied heavily on information provided by commercial companies. The large banks ran their own commercial intelligence organisations which regularly updated the Foreign Office and Board of Trade on economic trends abroad. Arms companies provided information on foreign contracts and on arms deals, particularly illicit arms trading. Lloyds Shipping maintained strong links to Naval Intelligence. Shell provided information on oil and other fuels, to the point that the SIS representative in Holland, Captain Payne Best, told German interrogators that he did not bother spying on German oil stocks. The Germans were convinced that Reuters regularly acted as a source of information. The American military attaché, Lieutenant Colonel Kenyon Joyce, wrote to his Government in 1927:

> I am convinced the British make more use of their nationals in various parts of the world for the collection of military information than we do. For instance I was recently informed that full data in regard to one of the railways in North China was submitted to the War Office by the British civilian engineer who built the road.

No doubt many businessmen who travelled abroad regularly were asked to keep an eye out for interesting information on their travels, or were gently questioned on their return. These men might not be spies in the accepted sense of the word, but could easily have crossed the line or laid themselves open to charges of spying if caught.

John Henry Leather – a British spy in France

John Leather was born in 1895 and served in the Royal Artillery during the First World War, remaining in the Army after the war with the Rhine Army Intelligence Corps. In 1925 he was arrested in France on espionage charges, denying any current connections with the British Army. The files (which show every sign of having been surreptitiously weeded) are in TNA's FO 371 series.

In December 1925 the Foreign Office learned of the arrest of three British subjects in France. Ernest Oliver Phillips, William Fischer and John Henry Leather were the Paris office staff of Burndept Wireless Ltd, and were accused of employing attractive young women to befriend French officers and to obtain information about aircraft and their dispositions.

Burndept Wireless agreed to pay the men's legal fees but on 5 January 1926 they wrote to the Foreign Office that they would not continue funding as 'there are some grounds for suspicion against Messrs Leather and Fischer'. When challenged, the company replied that 'certain facts have come to our knowledge which suggest that the responsibility for the expenses incurred does not really attach to this company'. Clearly they had discovered the secret-service connection.

The French press were delighted with the story. Extract from the *Petit Parisien*, 13 December 1925:

> William Fischer admitted that Marthe Moreuil was his friend. He made her acquaintance last March, shortly after his arrival in Paris, and, for eight days, he lived with her. Once Mrs. Fischer arrived in France in her turn, Marthe Moreuil went to live on her own, but relations continued between the Englishman and his friend.
>
> Did he give her money? He acknowledged that he had given her small gifts of items and money, but averred that this was not any kind of fixed monthly payment. In any case, the total was under 1,000 francs in cash, and Marthe Moreuil never received more than 400 francs in any single month.

Extract from the *Petit Parisien*, 17 December 1925:

During the war, (Leather said) I was an artillery lieutenant . . . after the armistice I belonged to the Intelligence Service Corps. I was in Cologne when, in 1924, I resigned my commission. Since then I have had no links with the Intelligence Service Corps and I have not committed any acts of espionage against France!

Why did the Englishman move around so much since arriving in France? It was, he maintained, simply a matter of organising the branch offices of his wireless telegraph company.

I was, (Fischer said) a sergeant in the counter-intelligence service at Cologne when I made Mr. Leather's acquaintance. After a time as a policeman in the Inter-Allied Commission for Upper Silesia, I returned to France to join the Rue de Surène wireless telegraph company. I also became Marthe Moreuil's friend, and I am convinced that she was spying on Mr. Leather's behalf.

On several occasions, I unexpectedly came across meetings between them. What were they saying to each other? I don't know, because they were talking in whispers, and I kept discreetly at some distance. But I believe that he was entrusting her with missions; and so it is that when my friend went off on her last journey, both Mr. Leather and I accompanied her to the station.

'All this is nothing but stories', Mr. Leather . . . 'I knew that Marthe Moreuil was my employee's friend; but I have never spoken a word to that woman, I have only seen her in bars with Fischer.'

A dancer named Andree Lefebvre also confessed to having spied for Leather himself, gathering information on the French Air Force. The women were sentenced to six months, with fines of 500 francs; Phillips and Fischer got two years with fines of 2,000 francs; but Leather received three years and a 3,000-franc fine. Clearly Leather was considered the ringleader.

The 1925 *Army List* includes J H Leather as a serving officer. The War Office list shows he was attached to MI2 (b), the War Office section dealing with intelligence on Western Europe (including France). Leather was also cousin of Desmond Morton, Head of Production for SIS. The two men's families were very close. Morton later took part in discussions with Admiral Sinclair and MI5 over the case of a Briton, Vivian Stranders, spying for Germany in Paris while pretending to spy for British intelligence. 'C' gave the opinion that 'there was very great danger of Stranders being arrested in France, and as he is a British subject, in C.S.S.'s opinion nothing would convince either the French Surete or the French public that he was not another LEATHER'.

Leather was released in May 1928 and returned to England. His Army career was over but he found employment at Woolwich Arsenal and became founder/manager of Bromley Little Theatre. He returned to the Army during the Second World War, becoming a Temporary Lieutenant Colonel, before leaving again after the war.

It is an interesting question why Britain should be spying on a close ally. Air Intelligence files from the period include AIR 5/573 'Mediterranean Air Menace – France' and AIR 9/20 'Directorate of Operations and Intelligence and Directorate of Plans:– France',

SIS agent John Henry Leather in relaxed mode in a Parisian night club. (with grateful thanks to Dr Simon Leather)

which reveal concern about the size of the French Air Services and their influence on British strategy in the Mediterranean. France also had the only sizeable air force capable of attacking the UK, so the Air Ministry was obliged to watch them. AIR 9/20 includes, from November 1925, a file 'Statement giving details by squadrons and machines of all aircraft belonging to the French Military and Naval Air Services'. The Air Staff were plainly interested in what the French were up to and were quite capable of asking SIS to obtain information about the perceived threat.

The Government Code & Cypher School

In 1919 Room 40 was amalgamated with Military Intelligence's MI1b and, as a cover, named the Government Code & Cypher School (GC&CS) under the control of the Director of Naval Intelligence. There was a legitimate and public role for the school – training servicemen in the use and creation of cyphers for the armed forces and government departments. Many staff from Room 40 joined GC&CS.

Behind this cover GC&CS concentrated on the interception and breaking of foreign cyphers, often with remarkable success. Early Russian codes (the Soviet government having stopped using the sophisticated Czarist codes) were particularly vulnerable. Japanese naval and many foreign diplomatic codes were broken. One significant failure, brought about through political interference and the revelation in Parliament that the British were reading

Soviet signals, was to break the later generation Soviet cyphers introduced in the late 1920s. CG&CS did have more success in breaking Comintern codes and the material was circulated under the codename 'MASK' and appears in KV 2 records of both Russian and British communists. GC&CS were also responsible for the intercepts that led to MI5 first becoming interested in Frederick Rutland and following his career as a Japanese spy.

In 1922 GC&CS was taken over by the Foreign Office and, when Admiral Sinclair became head of SIS, he also became Director of GC&CS and both organisations operated out of Broadway Buildings. GC&CS were effectively treated as being part of the secret service, but because of their overt role there are various lists of staff available in the FO 366 series and further releases in the HW and FO 1093 series, which mean that a good picture can be built up of who they were and what they did.

Among files worth examining are:

• FO 1093/104 – 'Code and Cypher School: establishment and recruitment of staff' – contains a handwritten list of initial staff, along with details of their salaries, ranks and dates of birth.

• FO 366/800 contains a complete staff list for GC&CS from 1922.

• FO 366/1024 contains a list of applicants for two posts at GC&CS in 1938, along with their qualifications and references.

• The HW 3 series contains various historical papers on GC&CS from the 1920s and 1930s including: HW 3/35 papers regarding the founding of GC&CS: along with applications by Room 40 staff to work in organisation and competing bids by Admiralty and War Office for senior posts; HW 3/40 covers GC&CS staff pay and conditions and there are other files relating to junior staff in the same series.

One of GC&CS's key staff was Ernest Constantine Fetterlein, a code-breaker for the Imperial Russian government who joined from Room 40 and his naturalisation papers are in HO 144/2848. HO 144/17120 and HO 144/17121 are the papers for his brother Paul, who also served at GC&CS and, presumably, Paul's son (also Paul).

With approach of war Admiral Sinclair began expanding GC&CS and purchased a property at Bletchley Park in Buckinghamshire as an evacuation station (known as Station X – Station 10) for the school. FO 366/2378 relates to the recruitment of emergency staff for the School, including lists of previous staff still available if necessary. There are also listed numerous academics at Oxford and Cambridge– one is J R R Tolkien of Pembroke College, Oxford (though he never took up a post).

The build up to the Second World War

During the mid and late 1930s the increasing threat from Nazi Germany led to more intelligence resources being employed against her, and to the threat of a new enemy, Germany's own intelligence services. By 1935 Italy and Japan were identified as likely enemies and SIS was ordered to establish organisations there, but given no more money to do so. In 1935 Sinclair asked for £500,000 to expand the service but was granted only £117,000. A recently released memo says:

> No big money was ever available until the spring of 1940 so the butter was spread very thinly. . . . Germany, Japan, Italy and Russia were potential enemies and all that existed was a rudimentary organisation depending on a limited number of passport-control offices and insufficient funds.

In spite of his recognised qualities, Sinclair was later accused of having been 'no good at choosing a staff. . . . the place was flooded with second and third rate, rather disgruntled retired Naval Officers and was a hot bed of jealousy, suspicion and intrigue'. One notable achievement came when Winterbotham, head of Section II, the Air Section, formed a secret high-altitude reconnaissance flight under cover of a private company. Successful flights were made over German and Italian targets, and even over the oilfields of southern Russia.

The 'Z' Network

A possible response to the increased workload and shortage of money was the creation in 1936 of the 'Z' Network under the control of veteran intelligence officer Claude Dansey, who had worked for MI5 and SIS during the First World War. Dansey set about recruiting new agents and assuming control of others. His agents were separate from those of the passport-control networks.

Dansey was, supposedly, dismissed from SIS for 'financial irregularities' and set about using business contacts to create his new network. Companies included Unilever, whose Swiss representative was a former First World War intelligence officer, Rex Pearson, and Royal Dutch Shell, both of whose London officers were on the Gestapo Black List. Alexander Korda, founder of London Films and film director and producer of note, was a prominent associate and there were many men in the diamond and oil businesses, as well as several journalists. Two of Dansey's agents have left detailed accounts of their work for him.

Conrad O'Brien-ffrench was a former First World War prisoner of war recruited by SIS in 1919 and sent to Sweden, working with Major Scale running agents into Russia. He continued with SIS under cover of running a ski school and holiday tours in Austria in the 1930s. His networks were subsumed into Dansey's organisation.

O'Brien-ffrench didn't like Dansey:

> on my first day Claude Dansey, as new chief, had insulted me by slipping me a fiver as if he were hooking a common informer. . . . during my six years of Hitler-watching over a large area of southern Germany, with many sub agents . . . I was receiving less pay than a window cleaner. . . . this and the fact that I discovered that my despatches were being forwarded to their appropriate destination without giving credit to their source, accentuated that sense of being alone and embattled.

Eventually O'Brien-ffrench was caught up in a raid on a meeting with an important German source and forced to flee, by night, in his sports car. At the Swiss border he had passed through the German barrier

> when some shots rang out behind me and I heard shouts of Halt! Halt! I put my foot down and almost failed to stop at the Swiss Control Point. . . . once I had reached the safety of Switzerland I began to realise that my hazardous activities were over.

Norman Dewhurst had worked for SIS in the Aegean in 1917 and the Baltic in 1920. By 1936 he had become an American citizen and was recruited by 'Our Man in New York' to return to Europe. After meeting Sinclair he went to the offices of Duveen and Co. on Kingsway where 'to my surprise, and our mutual satisfaction, I met my old chief Colonel Dansey'. Dansey sent Dewhurst into Italy to contact a former hotelier, Mr Monteggia, who had fallen foul of Mussolini.

Norman Dewhurst in Munich, 1937. An SIS officer in the First World War and immediately after, Dewhurst served as an agent in Germany before the Second World War and then in the Baltic States and Finland.

Dewhurst then investigated the building of a battleship at Genoa and reported on military movements and anti-aircraft defences.

Back in London he trained in 'lock picking, inks, codes, wireless telegraph, the photographing of documents (and) the organisation of the German Army with special reference to its different sections and to badges and other distinguishing markings'. He was given particular training in codes.

In Germany, posing as an author, he took an apartment in Munich, joined a hiking club and took a mistress. Through his network of friends (he was particularly extrovert and amicable) he picked up information on the German army, located airfields, obtained a map of the Munich garrison and a piece of light-weight alloy that he passed out through a courier. In late 1937 he was sent to Latvia, where his friendship with the German community led other British agents (unaware of his status) to report him as Germanophile. He recruited British residents as agents, spying on Germany and Russia. He remained after the 1940 Soviet occupation and was interviewed by their Secret Police who tried to recruit him to work for them in the USA. He moved to Finland, where he continued to work after they joined the Axis and was questioned by the Security Police. In early 1942 he persuaded the American Consulate to get him into Sweden from where he was flown to Britain.

Dewhurst cut his ties with SIS (after Dansey arranged return of his British citizenship) and ran a garage. He later joined the RAF and, after bumping into Dansey, was put in charge of the mess at a school training Free French officers to be dropped into Europe. He later returned to 'Special Duties', working in Belgium and on counter-intelligence in Germany after the war.

Developments in CX

During the late 1930s SIS changed its method of referencing its circulating CX material. In the same way that the Foreign Office had long given each country a unique number for ease of reference, so did SIS. Russia was now 95, Germany 12, Turkey 18 etc. The circulating sections retained their old numbers and these would follow the country number, so that a report on the Russian Air Force would be prefaced 952, on the German Navy 123. CX from a station abroad to Broadway would be sent as 120 from Berlin and from Head of Station as 12000, the 00 ('double o') identifying the Head. Later on, as stations expanded during the war, other station staff with specific functions were identified by individual numbers. Officers cleared for Ultra traffic seem to have a 700 designation, and Section V staff abroad to have adopted 500.

An Abwehr report on SIS

After the Second World War MI5 obtained Abwehr (German secret service) records concerning attempts to run double agents against SIS. KV 3/116 names several known SIS men and offers possibilities for further investigation, including some Germans allegedly working for SIS as agents.

German agent GV 152 had several contacts with SIS in The Hague from 1936 and from his reports the Germans first identified two British officers, HENDRICKS and CHITSON. Chitson should, in fact, be Chidson, who went on to establish SIS Section D. A further note identifies VRINTEN and MARTIN connected with the SIS in Holland.

Other documents name DALTON (who committed suicide), Lieutenant Colonel TEMPERLEY, who conducted the investigation into DALTON's death and HOOPER and TAYLOR, originally suspected of being involved in it. GV 152 also identified some German contacts of the British – KRAENEL or KROENEL from Duisberg and a Master Gunsmith Ignatz JAISEK, an Austrian from the Mauser Works at Oberndorf am Necker who frequented the station.

GV 152 also named RICHLEY (RIDHELEY?) from another passport-control office, who visited The Hague regularly; DANCY (actually our old friend Claude Dansey), correctly identified as Passport Control Officer in Rome; and CAMPBELL, said to hold a high position in Berlin and said to be number two to HOWARD.

Agent GVE 158 identified an English agent named PARKER a '40 – 45 year old gentleman . . . 1.75 tall, light grey-streaked hair, from accent seems to be a Dutchman' who had briefed him on a trial espionage mission into Germany.

German agent V M SCHULZKE contacted SIS in Belgium, who asked him for information on airfields and troop dispositions around Bremen and other towns. He was in contact with other alleged SIS agents. First was HEINRICH, identified as

an auxiliary waiter, Heinrich MAECHOLD, b 17.04.00 in Frankfurt/Main. . . . At the end of May M received 8 days leave and proposed extension of leave, to make a trip to Belgium. M is an evil and slanderous individual, whom the Kriminalpolizei in Frankfurt already have on record. M is being closely watched by the Stapo Frankfurt.

Second was JUPP, established as being Joseph LUSTER, a seaman who led the Gestapo to Anton VONES and TIEM. VONES was 'employed by Germania Werftin Kiel, in the section engaged on the construction of U boats for Turkey. TIEM is also employed in a marine workshop. LUSTER and VONES were arrested in June 1937 . . . on suspicion of espionage'.

In June 1935 the Abwehr fed information to an Englishman based in London, possibly a man named ELLIS, though MI5's notes suggest that they were linking him to the double agent SNOW, whose real name has not been officially released, though it is known to be OWENS. The notes quote a PF reference number PF 45241 OWENS and this PF reference is the same as appear on the SNOW KV 2 files KV 2/444 – KV 2/453.

The file lists three Englishmen suspected of being British agents in Innsbruck: Mr ILES, Mr SHERLOCK and Colonel GRAVES, as well as a language teacher whose name was unknown.

Other possible British agents mentioned are a Mr CALLINGHAM, who had approached a German regarding industrial metals, and a Mr Windsor BOWELL of the Thames Factory, Rainville Road, Hammersmith who contacted the same man.

In 1935 the Abwehr are known to have been providing 'chickenfeed' to the British Vice Consul Mr AUE, but by 1936 he had been transferred so the German plan to lead him on and have him arrested never came to fruition.

Another Englishmen who came under suspicion was Mr CRESSWELL, who in 1936 was 'wandering about on the Austrian German frontier, also in the Rhineland; he appeared to have made positive observations and to have travelled to London to make a personal report'. The Abwehr later received an SIS questionnaire from a double agent in touch with SIS in Berlin and they believed it had been derived in part from information gathered by CRESSWELL.

The Radio Security Service

Established in 1938, and run by the War Office with GPO assistance, the RSS looked for radio transmissions of German agents assumed to be working in Britain. RSS was offered to MI5, which felt unable to cover the expense on its limited budget, but was run by Lieutenant Colonel Adrian Simpson who had experience of radio work during the First World War. In addition to various fixed interception stations and mobile units, volunteer amateur interceptors were recruited among British radio hams. Though they did not locate any German agents (there were none), they did begin to pick up Abwehr transmissions from Europe which provided invaluable information about German agents coming to Britain. Because of the expertise that SIS had through their control of the GC&CS, the RSS organisation was transferred to them in 1941. Information gathered by the RSS was circulated in the form of highly secret messages known as ISOS.

Records of the RSS are in the HW 34 series and include, in HW 34/1, miscellaneous manuscript notes on its history.

Chapter 9

MI5 IN THE SECOND WORLD WAR

MI5 entered the Second World War better staffed and experienced than it went into the First World War, but its further expansion was as rapid and the public response to the war was every bit as hysterical – in fact with the fall of France MI5 threatened to collapse under the weight of its own investigations. The War Plan, drawn up in the late 1930s, had not anticipated imminent invasion and a struggling MI5 were even obliged to borrow staff from SIS.

Churchill forced Kell to retire in May 1940. He was replaced in the short term by Brigadier Oswald Harker and then by Sir David Petrie. In January 1941 MI5 was restructured to take some of the pressure off B Division, which now concentrated solely on espionage. A Division dealt with administration and the Registry; B Division dealt with espionage; C Division examined credentials; D covered security and travel control; E Division took over control of aliens and liaison with the counter-espionage services of refugee governments in Britain; F Division looked after subversive activities, including communists, fascists, pacifists and Jehovah's Witnesses.

Thanks to the work of the Radio Security Service and SIS Section V, which watched for enemy agents abroad, MI5 captured almost every German agent that came to Britain. Before the war MI5's Major Sinclair (born Reginald Teague-Jones, he had changed his name after being named as murderer of Russian Commissars at Baku during the Russian civil war) had done theoretical work on running double agents. Now Section B1a was established under Major T A (Tar) Robertson which controlled captured German agents after they had been interrogated at MI5's Camp 020. The double agents provided a carefully coordinated flow of false information to the Germans on everything from weather, troop movements and the build up to D-Day.

The Liddell diaries

An invaluable source of information on life within MI5, with occasional bits of scurrilous and salacious gossip thrown in, are the diaries of Guy Liddell, Head of B Division. These are in KV 4/185 to KV 4/196 and are available for download on TNA's website.

Beginning at the end of August 1939, the diaries run through twelve volumes to the end of June 1945. Each volume is indexed (though not in detail) so that it is reasonably easy to find references to members of staff. Liddell, of course, tended to deal with the more senior members of the service, though juniors are occasionally mentioned. He also dealt regularly with SIS, though the names of many of their officers have been redacted.

The diaries record Liddell's thoughts on such high-level plans as the blackmailing of German intelligence chief Admiral Canaris when he visited Portugal at the end of 1940 as: 'there is no doubt that he was in Russian pay', as well as the amusing 'Cecil has just discovered a Nun in this country who is writing in secret ink to a Priest in Ireland. It seems to be a love affair. The correspondence is merely obscene.'

MI5 agents

Maxwell Knight continued to run his deep-cover agents against both the rump of the British Union of Fascists and the Communist Party and there is a report on his section's work, detailing his most important cases and naming his additional staff, in KV 4/227 – 'Report on the work of M/S (agents) during the WW2'. Knight's agents can be identified in the files as they're prefixed by M, reporting on a wide range of suspects and subjects.

Other divisions ran their own agents against specific targets or groups. Regional security liaison officers (RSLO) had local contacts supplying information and occasionally used personal contacts of people they were interested in. Frederick Rutland was watched for Reading RSLO by Flight Lieutenant G E Daniel, who was billeted in the same house Rutland lived in, though Daniel probably did not count strictly as an agent.

Section E2 ran a Russian agent codenamed 'BRIT', who reported regularly on White Russians in Britain. A recently released Home Office file (HO 45/23692 – 'Silvio Mazarro, alias John Sylvester Maynard, alias Schonk, police informer: release from internment after intervention by security services') strongly suggests that he was employed by either MI5 or Special Branch as an informant among the Italian community.

Identifying anonymous double-cross Agents

The files on most of MI5's double agents have been released giving their real names. A small proportion remain anonymous because they have not previously identified themselves or given consent to be identified.

The vast majority of double-cross agents passed through Camp 020 for interrogation and KV 2/2593 ('List of cases investigated by Camp 020: chronological list of suspected spies investigated') provides a tool for identifying them. KV 2/2593 was reported to TNA as a means of breaking the agents' anonymity the day it was released, and subsequently exposed by BBC Radio 4's *Today* programme. Recalled by MI5, it was quietly returned to TNA without any redactions.

Agent SNIPER

Anonymous agent codenamed SNIPER was described as 'a pilot in the Belgian Air Force', who arrived in Britain in 1943. His heavily redacted file is KV 2/1138. An excerpt from the Camp 020 Monthly Summary for November 1943 in the file says:

> SNIPER is a Belgian subject aged 44. He arrived at the Belgian Consulate at San Sebastian on 11 9 43 and gave an account of contact with the Abwehr in Brussels and of a mission to this country . . . (Blank) was brought to this country with a view to interrogation at Camp 020.

KV 2/2593 lists four possible suspects. Two Belgians, Poils, alias Peker, and Pierre Charles Mompaey, entered Camp 020 at roughly the correct time. Two others are Hans Bertrand, who entered Camp 020 on 7 November 1943, and Hans Ruser, who entered on 23 November. Neither is stated as being Belgian.

Poils/Peker is described in KV 4/13 to KV 4/15 ('History of Camp 020') 'as a crooked Belgian stockbroker who found refuge from the law in the German secret service'. This does not fit SNIPER, who is referred to several times as a Belgian Air Force officer. Poils stayed in Camp 020 until 3 February 1945. Mompaey also remained in Camp 020 until 3 February 1945. We know that

SNIPER was released from Camp 020 in November 1943 because it is stated in the Camp 020 Monthly Summary for November 1943 that 'SNIPER has been released'.

Both Hans Bertrand and Hans Ruser were released to B1A, the MI5 section handling double agents. Ruser's release date was 17 December 1943 but Bertrand's was 15 November 1943, in time for his release to have been recorded in the Monthly Summary. In the Monthly Summary SNIPER's real name has been repeatedly redacted and the word SNIPER written in by hand in the space. Even allowing for over generous blanking of the name, it is not possible that Ruser would give enough space to allow for the insertion of SNIPER by hand. SNIPER has to be Hans Bertrand.

SNIPER/Bertrand passed the Germans out-of-date information on night fighters and false information on airfields before D-Day. In 1944 he went to Belgium and provided false information during the final weeks of the war.

Agent BEETLE

Double agent BEETLE is mentioned in *The Double Cross System in the War of 1939 to 1945* by J C Masterman. The Camp 020 History says he was an Icelandic refugee from Norway, arrested by American security officers in Iceland. Masterman says he was arrested in September 1943, having been landed from a U-boat.

On his arrival at Camp 020, Beetle's clothes and papers were examined but no hard evidence was found of espionage activity. He admitted to some contacts with German intelligence and the story of his journey to Iceland was palpably false. Lieutenant Colonel Stephens gave him a two-hour interrogation, at the end of which he confessed to having been blackmailed into espionage by the Germans over his black-market activities. He was to report on shipping and naval activities around Iceland. BEETLE confessed everything and 'The recommendation was, then, that {BEETLE} should be used as a double agent. He was returned to Iceland within six weeks of his admission to Camp 020.'

KV 2/2593 provides only one candidate that fulfils the criteria of arriving in Camp 020 in September 1943 and returning to Iceland within six weeks. Tomsen Friedriksson arrived on 29 September 1943 and was deported to Iceland on 13 November. There is a note that his personal file (PF 65987) was destroyed on 18 May 1963. Presumably, as a double agent working abroad, BEETLE counts as an SIS agent – certainly his colleague COBWEB, also operating in Iceland, was run by SIS.

Seaman agents

MI's Section B1L ran an extensive network of agents aboard British and Allied merchant ships and airlines. They watched British seamen in neutral ports and tried to plant false information on German agents abroad. Initial plans were to run hundreds of agents and some 350 were recruited, but the operation was scaled down and later ran a much smaller number of seamen.

Agents were run by the MI5 port officers at Newcastle, Liverpool, Glasgow and Cardiff, with a head office in London headed by Mr Stopford. Agents were generally given a woman's name as a codename and the officers a number (Stopford was 4000 and Mr Wilkie at Liverpool 2000).

Several important double-agent cases came out of B1L, a couple of important German agents were detected by them and vital work was done in closing gaps in the censorship and preventing smuggling of letters to Eire. Several agents were passed over to SIS for further work.

There are two main files on B1L, the first of which, KV 4/163 – 'B1L functions 1941–1945' – has been particularly badly weeded, in that it contains details that should allow a dedicated researcher to be able to identify some of the agents, and even an unredacted list of returning agents from September 1942.

William Armstrong	SS *Bendoran*
Edgar Beamey	SS *City of Cardiff*
William Herbert Howard	SS *Nebraska*
Alexander McCormick	SS *Nariva*
Leslie McCardle	SS *Baron Yarborough*
Andrew Unsworth	SS *City of Marseilles*
William Lewis	SS *Daldorch*
Charles Taylor	SS *Kingsbury*
John Joseph Corner	SS *Empire Moon*
Auguste Frans Goris	SS *Mafuta*
Kreal Joseph Aetrts	SS *Mafuta*
Halfdan Strom	SS *Arosa*
Mario Piqueras Mori	SS *Coracero*
Hubert Hargreaves	SS *David Livingstone*

There are some curious aspects to the record in that TNA's website says of the files on double agent 'JOSEF' (KV 2/2267 – KV 2/2276): 'JOSEF was the only UK-based Double Agent run by the Security Service against the Japanese . . . He established contact with Japanese military and naval intelligence in Lisbon as a result of his association with the Japanese honorary Press Attaché in London.'

KV 4/163 mentions 'JOSEF' several times but also: 'The other agent working against the Japanese is WENDY who is now handled in London'. A note from December 1943 says:

> we have developed another line to the Japanese in Lisbon through our agent WENDY, who is also a Russian seaman, and appears, so far, to have gone satisfactorily and had provided valuable confirmatory evidence connected with the cases of JOSEF and SPARK.

Clearly more than one double was being used. Other descriptions of agents are surely precise enough to allow the agent to be identified? 'CHLOE' is:

> aged 22, is a good type, a gentleman and an intelligent person . . . unjustifiably sentenced to three years imprisonment by court martial in East Africa where he had a commission with the K A R in September 1941. The sentence was subsequently remitted and in January, 1943, he was recruited by B1L as he had previous merchant navy experience. . . . He came to this country, and was instructed in conjunction with SIS for the task of penetrating the BRANDES organisation in Lisbon.

Agent 'GLADWYS' was:

> A Welshman aged about 22 . . . obtained a war degree at Jesus College, Oxford . . . rather left wing in politics and, at our instigation became a member of the WELSH NATIONALIST PARTY, which he penetrated with considerable success. Speaks French, Spanish and Norwegian fluently and has a moderate knowledge of Italian, Portuguese, German and Swedish.

Several agents were women, particularly those connected with the aviation industry. 'JOSEPHINE' was 'A very astute British agent in touch with all the Swedish Airline personnel flying between Stockholm and Dyce.' 'EILEEN' was a 'recently recruited British agent in the Swedish airlines office who supplies copies of confidential correspondence concerning that office. She also knows various junior members of the Swedish legation.'

A 6-monthly report on B1L for the first half of 1943 says 87 old agents have been dropped, 2 have lost their lives and 11 new agents taken on. It may be a coincidence, but the Passport Register for April 1943 shows that William J Thomas, William H Perry, Ernest Jebbett, Henry Harper, Herbert F Hall, Leslie C Fielder, John A Drewry, William F Davies, Joseph Kerley, John Brennan and Arthur Londsdale all received Box 500 gratis passports. Attempts to trace the men as MI5 officers travelling abroad on business have come to nothing and the working hypothesis is that they were B1L agents. Certainly an Ernest Jebbett and Joseph Patrick Kerley show as having been merchant seamen when their names are put through TNA's online database of merchant seamen medals.

Other places to find MI5 documents

Detainees

On MI5's recommendation many foreign aliens and Britons suspected of being in favour of the enemy or against the war on ideological grounds (such as pacifists) were interned. Many of the aliens were Jews and other genuine anti-Nazis, and many Britons considered themselves nothing more than genuine patriots, and their appeals and other documents relating to their detention are in the Home Office papers.

HO 283 contains the papers of Sir Norman Birkett QC, who headed the appeals committee, and many detainees' records. Some of these have been open for years, but others have only been released relatively recently through Freedom of Information requests. They include Captain Robert Cecil, a prominent member of the British Union of Fascists, 1934–1938, and Defence Regulation 18B detainee Joseph Anthony Donohoe, whose files were released in 2005. Many of these HO 283 records are linked on TNA's database to other related records, usually in the HO 45 series.

Personal files on some 86 detainees are available in HO 214/84, though over 800 people were detained so presumably further records lurk within the Home Office system.

It is also worth checking the HO 45 series for material. If nothing else these are likely to contain MI5 references. HO 45/25751 contains copies of letters to his MP from Cecil Allchurch, detained in the Isle of Man. A letter to the Home Office, dated 24 May 1942, about his correspondence comes from S H Noakes whose position is not immediately obvious until you realise that the letter is headed PO Box 500, Oxford and has the reference PF.49156/F3c1. PO Box 500 has long been an MI5 cover address and PF.49156/F3c1 presumably refers to Allchurch's MI5 personal file, with F3c1 being the section that was dealing with him. F3 section dealt with 'Right Wing and nationalist Movements – British Union, Scots Nationalists, German and Austrian Right Organisations and Pro-Nazi Individuals.'

If you have an ancestor who was detained during the war but are unable to find records for them by using TNA's search engine then a Freedom of Information request to the Home Office might be useful – email:

public.enquiries@homeoffice.gsi.gov.uk; write: Home Office, Direct Communications Unit, 2 Marsham Street, London SW1P 4DF. You will need to explain exactly what you are looking for and request that documents are placed in the public domain. You will probably need to prove that the subject of your enquiry is dead or, if still alive, you have their authority. You may need to be both patient and persistent.

Foreign Office records

The presence of so many governments in exile in Britain, with their attendant groups of refugees, kept MI5 E Division busy throughout the war. There are occasional MI5 political reports dealing with these governments and their policies scattered through the FO 371 series. One such is a report on Polish–Lithuanian relations in FO 371/43051.

SIME – Security Intelligence Middle East

SIME handled security in the Mediterranean in collaboration with MI5 and SIS Section V. An MI5 officer posted to SIME HQ in Cairo liaised with them about information received from RSS about enemy agents. MI5 officers and Registry staff were loaned to SIME and visits made by officers with expertise in port control, counter-sabotage, investigation techniques and security measures. SIME officers worked closely with the Turkish secret service and with French services in Syria. SIME ran a number of successful double-agent operations in the Middle East and the Mediterranean. Most of SIME's files were destroyed after the war.

Most surviving files so far released are in the KV series, though there are some reports and summaries in WO 204 series, including WO 204/12966 – 'Personalities: SIME (Security Intelligence Middle East) enquiries in AFHQ and Middle East Forces', WO 204/8854 – 'Security Intelligence Middle East reports on Greece' and WO 204/12963 – 'SIME (Security Intelligence Middle East) summaries'.

Among the KV series are KV 4/234 – KV 4/237 dealing with the role and development of the organisation, KV 4/197 dealing with SIME's Special Section running double and triple agents against the Abwehr, KV 4/304 – KV 4/307 containing papers on SIME and the Middle East Intelligence Centre and KV 4/240 a report on SIME by a senior MI5 officer from 1943. There are KV 2 files on some SIME double agents including KV 2/1133 'CHEESE' – an invaluable deception agent – and KV 2/1281 – KV 2/1285 'KISS' – a double agent run in cooperation with the Soviet intelligence service.

Chapter 10

OTHER INTELLIGENCE AND SECRET ORGANISATIONS IN THE SECOND WORLD WAR

The Home Guard Auxiliary Units

The Auxiliary Units were the clandestine sabotage units created in Britain after Dunkirk in 1940. Many of their officers already had intelligence connections or went on to serve in Special Operations Executive (SOE) or elsewhere.

As Dunkirk was being evacuated SIS Section D Officers began recruiting 'clergymen, game-keepers, poachers, dentists and road-menders in defence of their country'. They started their work in early June 1940 and by late July had appointed nearly 200 key men and established 1,000 dumps of explosives and incendiaries.

A key officer involved in setting up the 'Auxiliary Units' was Ian Fleming's brother Peter, who was working for the War Office. One intelligence officer was the actor Anthony Quayle. Both Fleming and Quayle later transferred to SOE and their SOE files have both been released. Another interesting release has been the file on an original Section D officer, Captain G F S Sutton, who was employed 'June '40 – Auxiliary Units – Laying down secret arms dumps in England in case of invasion' (HS 9/1430/3).

The main role of the Auxiliary Units (who wore Home Guard uniforms as cover for their activities) was to be sabotage of invading German troops. Their headquarters was at Coleshill House near Swindon. The Auxiliaries were trained in unarmed combat, handling explosives and night scouting.

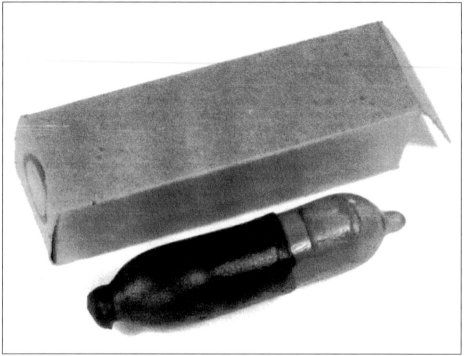

One of many sabotage devices produced for the Auxiliary Units, the Tysule contained a mix of petrol and paraffin and was to be used as an incendiary device. (courtesy of Norma Bonney)

Connected with them, and probably organised by SIS, were the even more secret Special Duties Sections, and members of these were trained to act as spies behind German lines if they ever landed and got established.

There are three lists of men who served in the Auxiliary Units in TNA files WO 199/3388, WO 199/3389 and WO 199/3390. WO 199/3391 is a handwritten register of men who served in the southern counties. These lists do not include members of the Special Duties Section.

A museum dedicated to Britain's wartime resistance organisation was established at Parham in Suffolk in 1997. The museum has over 200 photographs of original patrols, which might aid relatives trying to find out if an ancestor served, as well as over 40 tape recordings of veterans' reminiscences. They also have an extensive network of contacts throughout the country who are experts on patrols in their own local area. The Museum is always keen to hear from former auxiliaries and their relatives.

Naval Intelligence

During the Second World War Naval Intelligence was vitally important in gathering and collating material. It enjoyed a close, though not always amicable, relationship with SIS and relied far more on it for information than it had in the First World War. It was particularly scathing of SIS's inability to provide accurate and up-to-date information on the movements of German shipping. The naval attaché in Sweden ran his own coast-watching network which reported on movements in the Baltic direct to NID. He also cultivated a number of sources, including the Roumanian attaché who provided information against his own German allies. SIS did source good information on U-boat construction and later in the war had built up good coast-watching networks of its own, particularly in Norway. Many of the Naval Intelligence centres established during the First World War were still operational and a continuous stream of data was sent in by them.

Perhaps the most famous Naval Intelligence officer was Ian Fleming, who was a personal assistant to Director Admiral Godfrey. ADM 223/490 includes papers on 'Goldeneye' (precautions against German invasion of Spain) and correspondence with Fleming himself. 'Goldeneye' was a secret plan drawn up by the three armed services to commit sabotage in Spain and was later taken over by SOE. The name of the operation so impressed Fleming that he later named his house in Jamaica after it.

Fleming established a top-secret commando unit (30 Commando, later called 30 Assault Unit and 30 Advanced Unit or Special Engineering Unit). Trained in safe-breaking, special fighting techniques, demolitions, search techniques and photography, the men of the unit landed in North Africa, in Sicily and at D-Day. Working ahead of advancing troops, they captured hundreds of important German secret documents, a score or so valuable German research scientists and top-secret equipment. A detachment also served in the Far East. Unit records have been released including: DEFE 2/1107, which includes medal recommendations; ADM 202/308, containing reports and staff lists; ADM 223/214, the Unit History; and ADM 223/349 and ADM 223/501, which include lists of the unit's targets. The War Diary for March 1944 to June 1945 is in WO 218/71.

NID records from the Second World War are in ADM 223 series.

Air Intelligence

In the 1920s and 1930s Air Intelligence was conducted by the Directorate of Operations and Intelligence but on the outbreak of war a separate

Directorate of Intelligence was created. It was greatly enlarged in 1941 and a scientific section was created. AI 1(c) was the liaison section with SIS, both in setting out questions for their agents and also providing aircraft for the dropping and recovery of agents.

Air Intelligence files are in AIR 40 series, the vast majority of the over 3,000 records coming from the Second World War and later. They include technical assessments of aircraft, appreciations of bombing raids, reports of raids, photographs and interrogation reports of prisoners of war. There are other Air Intelligence papers in other AIR series – AIR 20/1718 contains a lecture by Dr R V Jones, Assistant Director of Intelligence (Science) on SIS and its relations with Air Intelligence.

There are several files relating to RAF/SIS/SOE agent-dropping operations in the AIR 20 series.

AIR 40/2572 contains notes on *The 'Oslo Evidence': scientific intelligence sent covertly to British Naval Attache, Oslo, Nov 1939* by R V Jones.

The Intelligence Corps

There seems to have been less planning for field intelligence work before the Second World War than there was before the Frist World War. Major (later Field Marshal Sir) Gerald Templar trained special security sections, allowing the BEF to deploy to France with trained field-intelligence units. By the end of the war the Corps had over 3,000 officers and nearly 6,000 other ranks. The Intelligence Corps was formally created on 15 July 1940.

Fortunately for the family historian with a relative in the Corps, much more information is available about individuals and their work than in the First World War. Though service records have not been released they are at least available through the Army Records Centre in Glasgow and the Corps Museum also holds much information.

Many of the roles played by the Corps were similar to the ones played in the First World War: interrogation of prisoners of war, examination of captured documents, photographic interpretation, field security and signals intelligence. In the latter case, Intelligence Corps Wireless Intelligence Sections were attached to Royal Signals Special Wireless Sections operating sometimes very close to the front line. They analysed the pattern of enemy transmissions as well as noting their messages for sending to Bletchley Park for breaking. At Bletchley some 40 per cent of the Army personnel wore Intelligence Corps badges and Corps radio personnel manned many of the out stations that collected German radio traffic. Formed specifically for duty with the airborne forces, 89 FSS saw action in North Africa, Sicily, Italy,

Greece, France, Belgium, Holland and Norway. Of sixteen officers and men who went into the battle at Arnhem only three made it back to Britain.

After the war, in both Germany and the Far East, the Intelligence Corps played a prominent part in rounding up war criminals. Corps members were directly involved in the arrest of Heinrich Himmler as he tried to slip past a road block at Bremervoerde.

In addition to their regular military role the Corps provided many men to assist the more secret intelligence organisations. MI5's Anthony Blunt and John Masterman, the Oxford academic who developed the 'Double Cross' system, both wore the Corps badge. Many of MI5's port and travel-control officers were also Corps members. When the Security Service needed two men to keep a close eye on the double agent 'Zig Zag' they employed two former policemen, Allan Tooth and Paul Backwell, both Corps NCOs, to live with him, befriend him and watch him.

SOE would frequently badge an agent as Intelligence Corps in the hope that having at least a semblance of military rank might protect them from being shot as spies. Harry Ree, who worked in Alsace and who arranged with the owners of a Peugeot factory to sabotage their own plant, was nominally an Intelligence Corps officer. It is probable that SIS did the same.

War diaries

As in the First World War, many Intelligence Corps men served on attachment to headquarters of other units, but some Field Security Sections, Censor Sections, Amplifier Units, Interpreter Sections, Port Security Sections and Special Wireless Sections have left War Diaries. The Diaries are at TNA but are held by the 'theatre' (or part of the world) that the unit was in. It is possible, therefore, that if a unit served in the Expeditionary Force to France in 1939, then in the UK after Dunkirk, was sent to North Africa and later served in France after D-Day that you will have to search several theatres to piece together the unit's whole history.

War Diaries can be found using TNA's search engine. 86 Port Security Section's Diary covering June 1942 to March 1943 (when they were in North Africa) is in WO 175/1280, the diary for 1 Base Censor Unit covering January to October 1945 (in Italy) are in WO 170/7153.

There is a comprehensive Order of Battle for Intelligence Corps units showing their movements throughout the war in WO 212/506.

The Intelligence Corps Museum

The Intelligence Corps Museum at Chicksands has a complete card index of

Intelligence Corps other ranks. These cards include some information about previous units served in, Corps units served in along with dates of posting as well as date of discharge or posting to another corps or regiment. Please note that these records will only be released to the serviceman or his next of kin. The museum also holds general details of officers' commissions and promotions. They have a complete Roll of Honours and Awards to Corps members from 1940 to date. Two excellently researched and compiled collections list all Corps members who served with SOE and MI5 during the war, along with some details of their services to these organisations and further references.

MI9 and IS9

Many thousands of prisoners of war in Germany and elsewhere, or those who managed to evade capture and get home, owed much to a secret service dedicated to helping them and to collecting intelligence from them. MI9 was formed in December 1939 under Major (later Brigadier) Norman Crockatt. Its charter made it responsible for the preparation and execution of plans for facilitating the escape of British prisoners, for arranging instructions in escape and evasion techniques, for making advance provisions for escapes, for collecting information from prisoners and for advising on counter escape measures against German prisoners of war escaping. Within seven months of Dunkirk MI9 had established contact with all the prisoner-of-war camps in Germany. Prisoners were encouraged to organise escape committees, to appoint code and intelligence officers and to prepare for escapes.

Most of MI9's work was open and above board. Its officers gave lectures to service personnel on escape and evasion techniques. MI9 officers also interrogated escaped prisoners of war about their experiences and their reports are scattered through the WO and AIR series.

Number 9 Intelligence School – MI9's secret service

IS9 was formed in January 1942 to facilitate escapes from prisoner-of-war camps and gather and collate intelligence in support of escapes. Its members sent and received coded messages from the camps, sent in special escape equipment and assisted the escape lines that ran right across Europe. It was organised in the following way:

- IS9 (W) interrogated all escaped or repatriated prisoners as well as those who had evaded capture. It also prepared and circulated all the reports and internal correspondence.

- IS9 (X) was responsible for escape and evasion planning, collecting information on the location of prisoner-of-war camps, preparing escape maps and selecting, recording and coordinating the sending of escape equipment into camps.
- IS9 (Y) prepared coded messages to camps, liaised with outside secret departments, corresponded with the camps, kept in touch with relatives of select prisoners of war, decoded and passed on messages received from camps, kept records on all escapers, attempted escapers and their helpers, dealt with censorship slips, special questionnaires and interviewed special escapers.
- IS9 (Z) prepared and developed escape equipment, prepared parcels to be sent to prisoner-of-war camps and equipment and clothing for agents being sent into the field. IS9 (Z) created miniature tools and compasses sent into prisoner-of-war camps in food parcels. Red Cross parcels were never used in case the Germans discovered them and stopped their delivery. A whole series of fake organisations and individuals were created from whom the parcels were supposed to come.
- IS9 (D) sent agents into the field and arranged for the picking up of escapers or evaders from occupied Europe. It was firmly under the control of SIS but only covered Western Europe and in other parts of the continent MI9 had a freer hand. N Section (covering the Mediterranean area) ran its own agents into the Balkans and western desert, including a number of Jewish agents dropped into Hungary and Czechoslovakia.

SIS established the first escape network operating from Portugal, through Spain into Vichy France, under the control of Donald Darling, who had the codename 'Sunday' and cover as a vice consul. The escape line was arranged by the ubiquitous Claude Dansey and it was him that recruited as London contact Jimmy Langley, a young Guards officer who had lost an arm at Dunkirk, escaped from a German military hospital and made his way to Vichy France under his own initiative. After reaching Marseilles he had worked with an escape line before he was repatriated in 1941. Langley's father had been an SIS agent and counter-Bolshevism officer in Switzerland in 1919.

Langley's new organisation was known as IS 9(D) or P15 section of SIS. It struggled in the face of apparent SIS apathy, if not hostility, relying on SIS contacts with the intelligence organisations of refugee governments for recruitment of its first agents. SIS provided radio training for IS9D's agents as well as in codes and parachuting but frequently interfered with operations that it thought might interfere with their own intelligence-gathering priorities.

Langley was joined by Captain Airey Neave (codenamed 'Saturday'), who had escaped from Colditz. Together they looked after the escape organisations that had sprung up across Europe, from Holland down through Belgium, France and into Spain. Radio operators and organisers were sent in, usually by parachute, to help them and occasionally to start new lines. Their escape lines led mainly into neutral Spain, though some men were brought out from Brittany by small boat.

As D-Day approached it became harder to pick up escapees from Europe and an audacious plan was hatched to gather them together in a French forest and keep them supplied and looked after by the French Resistance for collection after the invasion. Following D-Day Neave and Langley went to France and were attached to Supreme Headquarters Allied Expeditionary Force (SHAEF) as IS9 (WEA) with explicit instructions from Crockatt that they were not to become a 'private army'. As soon as the Americans broke out of the peninsula IS9 (WEA) fanned out to locate prisoners. Airey Neave, a few IS9 (WEA) jeeps and an SAS Squadron liberated nearly 150 evaders from their hiding place near Le Mans. When the Arnhem operation in Holland broke down in September IS9 (WEA) men were able to organise escape routes across the Rhine for the many paratroops who had gone into hiding among the Dutch population.

Much of its work later in the war, in addition to continuing to aid escapers and evaders, consisted of drawing up emergency plans, which thankfully did not have to be used, to drop SAS or Jedburgh teams into prisoner-of-war camps if the SS, as expected, began shooting prisoners. IS9 teams also visited camps seeking their own captured agents.

Files on MI9 and IS9 are scattered throughout the HS and WO series.

WO 208/3242 contains the history of IS9 with brief descriptions of the various sections and their work. It also contains structure charts of the organisation and lists of officers (including women) who had served.

WO 208/3246 is a history of IS9 in Western Europe, including a structure chart for the organisation in April 1945 with names and postings of officers.

WO 208/3250 is a history of IS9 in the Mediterranean with details of operations.

There are MI9 files specific to RAF prisoners of war and escapees in AIR 40/1932 and AIR 40/1933, and other files relating to the organisation can be found in AIR 40/2450 and 2451, covering the Far East, and HS 7/172 and 173, which cover the Eastern Mediterranean.

Other files in WO 208 include details of the organisation, some staff files and copies of reports. There are hundreds of escape and evaders reports between WO 208/3298 and WO 208/3327.

There are individual files on some of MI9's Palestinian organisation staff and agents between WO 208/3401 and WO 208/3415. Included are Hanna Szenes (WO 208/3401), who parachuted into Yugoslavia in 1943 was captured, tortured and killed, and Noah Nussbacher (WO 208/3405), who was on the same mission and was also captured and tortured but managed to escape and worked as a radio operator in Budapest before eventually reporting to the British Military Mission after the city fell to the Russians.

KV 2/728 – KV 2/741 contain MI5's files on Stella Lonsdale, who was in contact with the 'Pat' line for German intelligence, and KV 2/415 – KV 2/417 contain MI5's records on Harold Cole, who helped escaping British servicemen reach safety but then betrayed an MI9 escape line resulting in the deaths of over fifty people.

British Army Aid Group

Formed after the fall of Hong Kong, British Army Aid Group (BAAG) carried out MI9 work from China directed at Japanese prisoner-of-war camps in the colony. It provided medical help, escape gear and advice to escapees from Hong Kong and pilots who had been shot down and were on the run, and also gathered intelligence on Japanese activities.

Its commander was an Australian doctor, Lindsay Tasman Ride, who had escaped from Hong Kong and who was made a colonel and appointed MI9's representative in May 1942.

By May 1945 BAAG had assisted to freedom 130 British and Americans, 350 Indians and thousands of Chinese. From mid-1944 it carried out propaganda work in Hong Kong directed at all non-Japanese there. It had a small counter-espionage section consisting of two officers, one British and one Indian, as well as a Chinese solicitor and a Chinese businessman. It established hospitals for Chinese and distributed food for famine relief, rice for planting and took care of dependants of Chinese serving in British forces. Its relief work gave it excellent cover for clandestine work assisting escaped prisoners and shot-down aircrew. At the end of the war BAAG played an important role in the reoccupation of the colony after Japan's surrender.

SIS circulated the intelligence gathered by BAAG in CX form but acknowledged the source in doing so. A CX dated 9 July 1945 reported on numbers of Chinese labourers employed in Kowloon docks as well as on the manufacture of armaments in the dockyard workshops.

Records of BAAG are split between War Office (WO) and SOE (HS) series:

HS 1/167 contains a partial nominal role, listing mainly officers but a few other ranks who served as drivers and radio operators. A further list is in HS 8/991.

WO 208/747 is a BAAG report on conditions in Hong Kong: from March 1945. There are copies of some of their intelligence reports in WO 208/222, WO 208/451, WO 208/451, WO 208/452A and WO 208/452B. WO 208/425 is a report on their famine-relief work. There are reports BAAG's activities in WO 203/5208 and WO 203/5766.

After Colonel Ride's death in 1977, his widow donated his BAAG files to the Australian War Memorial, who presented the Ministry of Defence with the microfiche copies now held in WO 343.

Phoneys – hiding 'Enemy Aliens'

A rich source of agents for both SOE and SIS, and the basis for a unique group of Special Service soldiers known as 3 Troop, No. 10 (Inter Allied Commando), were the large numbers of foreign refugees, particularly German and Austrian dissidents (including many Jews), who had escaped from Europe. The employment of 'enemy aliens' created numerous problems with security and, of course, for the aliens themselves in the event they were captured on operations.

The only branch of the services enemy aliens could serve in was the Pioneer Corps, which became a recruiting ground for Special Forces, SIS and SOE. In order to try and protect them, and any families left behind, from reprisals, they were given false identities and a whole new Army Record that would stand up to close scrutiny by the enemy.

The War Office devised a secret procedure whereby foreign soldiers could be disguised. On notification from the War Office the Army Record Office at Ashford issued phoney names and numbers and false documents were prepared and forwarded to the man's new unit. From the surviving list of 'phoneys' it appears that most men adopted a British name but maintained the same initials as they had previously so that Private 13801228 A V ARMSTEIN became Private 13118501 A V ANDERSON. The man's true documents were retained under secret cover and the false documents put into normal circulation. Careful precautions were taken to ensure that no link could be made between the 'old' and the 'new' number. If a man was later transferred back to the Pioneer Corps then his 'old' record was suitably

DISCOVER MORE ABOUT MILITARY HISTORY

Pen & Sword Books have over 1500 titles in print covering all aspects of military history on land, sea and air. If you would like to receive more information and special offers on your preferred interests from time to time along with our standard catalogue, please complete your areas of interest below and return this card (no stamp required in the UK). Alternatively, register online at www.pen-and-sword.co.uk. Thank you.

PLEASE NOTE: We do not sell data information to any third party companies

Mr/Mrs/Ms/Other.................Name.....................................

Address..

....Postcode.................

Email address..

if you wish to receive our email newsletter, please tick here ❑

PLEASE SELECT YOUR AREAS OF INTEREST

Ancient History ❑	Medieval History ❑	English Civil War ❑
Napoleonic ❑	Pre World War One ❑	World War One ❑
World War Two ❑	Post World War Two ❑	Falklands ❑
Aviation ❑	Maritime ❑	Battlefield Guides ❑
Regimental History ❑	Military Reference ❑	Military Biography ❑

Website: www.pen-and-sword.co.uk • Email: enquiries@pen-and-sword.co.uk
Telephone: 01226 734555 • Fax: 01226 734438

Pen & Sword Books
FREEPOST SF5
47 Church Street
BARNSLEY
South Yorkshire
S70 2BR

amended so that any reference to special service was removed and the 'old' documents were put back into circulation. In the event of a man's death Ashford would carry out the necessary documentation in the false name, including notification of next of kin

Though most of the men whose identities were changed were from No. 10 (Inter Allied Commando), it seems likely that both SOE and SIS used the same procedures in order to 'sanitise' their own agents before they were sent into the field. Certainly the title of the main file (see below) that deals with the procedure suggests this is the case.

In 1946 the Combined Record Office at Ashford compiled a list of all the 'phoneys' they could trace in their records and the lists are available at TNA in file WO 106/6155 'Pioneer Corps Records (SOE)'. Unfortunately, as they explained in their covering letter, 'although the index is large, the information is relatively small. In many cases all that is known is that a certain Army Number was allotted to a certain man'.

The Gestapo Handbook and Black List, 1940

An interesting potential source identifying British agents from the beginning of the Second World War is the Gestapo Black List (*Sonderfahndungsliste GB*) for the invasion of Britain in 1940. Compiled for SS General Walter Schellenberg, it is a list of people wanted for questioning by the directorate of Reich Security (*Reichssicherheitshauptamt*) or RSHA and a general guide to the constitution, institutions, industries and population of Great Britain. Among the institutions discussed are the intelligence service and the Germans show both a profound ignorance and, occasionally, some deep knowledge of their opposition.

They certainly identified the existence of SIS, though were confused as to whether it really was the secret service and identified MI5 and its counter-espionage function, but thought it was part of Scotland Yard. The Germans also acknowledged the existence of the intelligence sections of the armed forces and of Special Branch.

Much of the information about SIS came from the interrogations of Captain Sigismund Payne Best and Major Richard Stevens, captured by the Germans at Venlo in Holland in November 1939. Between them they provided a rudimentary structure for SIS (getting the section numbers confused), a list of names and some explanation of SIS's workings. The Germans now had their suspicions about the passport-control organisation confirmed, as well as learning about the existence of the 'Z' Network and

Section D. Stevens told his captors that this was 'headed by Colonel Grand and his assistant Lieutenant-Colonel M R Chidson (formerly PCO in The Hague)'. Stevens also advised that several SIS sections had moved to Bletchley and Best gave the address of the 'Z' Network at Bush House, Aldwych, as well as the names of Dansey's assistants.

One of the most worrying inclusions (had MI5 known about it) was the following comment:

> Captain King's office is at 308 Hood House, Dolphin Square, using the name Coplestone, which is a cover for MI5. It is here that MI5 briefs and debriefs its contacts. Capt King lived at Whitehall Mansions and his official office was located at the War Office.

Captain King was one of Maxwell Knight's aliases. Coplestone was Knight's second wife's maiden name and the flat was in her brother's name. This was the most secret of MI5's operations, involving deep-cover agents in both the communist and fascist movements, but there is no explanation of where the Germans obtained their information. It is extremely unlikely it came from Payne Best or Stevens – most probably it came from one of Knight's contacts within the BUF who had gone to Germany – perhaps even William 'Lord Haw Haw' Joyce himself.

MI5 Officer Maxwell Knight with one of his less exotic pets – in later life he was the BBC's 'Uncle Max' and presented wildlife programmes. (via Bryan Clough)

The Special Wanted List GB itself

The Special Wanted List names 2,820 individuals, though there are a few who appear more than once. James McGuirk Hughes, prominent member of Moseley's BUF (and MI5 agent), is in under his correct name, together with three aliases.

Most of the people are mentioned in the list for political reasons (Churchill, Chamberlain and Attlee), as well as prominent pacifists, socialists and liberals. There are numerous Jewish refugees and individuals such as Noel Coward, Virginia Woolf and the cartoonist David Low.

A number of people are included because of possible connections with secret-service organisations. Many were derived from the interrogation of Payne Best and Stevens, but others were probably the result of other intelligence. Claude Dansey is mentioned as 'Brit Hauptagent, London' (British Head Agent, London), Norman Dewhurst is '9.8.87, Southport, brit ND , Schriftsteller, zuletz Riga, jetz London' (British secret service, writer, last at Riga, now in London), Frank Foley is 'Folley, Frank Edward, Kapitan, ehemaliger, Leiter d. brit. Passburos in Berlin, vermutl, England' (Captain, formerly head of British Passport Bureau, Berlin believed to be in England). There is a possible mention of Desmond Morton as 'Morton, brit Major, vermutl England (Taterkreis: Oberst Gibson)' (believed to be in England (spy ring Colonel Gibson). The Germans had identified connections between Passport Control and British intelligence and sought several passport-control officers.

There are virtually no MI5 officers referred to. In spite of knowing that he had only recently retired, Kell is not mentioned in the list itself or Holt-Wilson, his deputy, or Guy Liddell, who is actually included elsewhere in the handbook. Hinchley-Cooke is mentioned as being 'Leiter von MI5

An early cartoon of Hinchley-Cooke, First World War. He is mentioned in the Gestapo Black List of 1940 as being 'Leiter von MI5 (Military Intelligence)' and described a follows: 'wears glasses, is robust, fresh-faced, appears to be good natured and speaks German fluently in a mix of dialects from Saxony and Hamburg'. Hinchley-Cooke joined MI5 as a civilian early in the First World War and was quite well known as an MI5 spokesman before the Second World War. (from the MI5 cartoon book *Secrets of Waterloo(se) House*)

Our Lt. W. H. C. is authorised to take official photographs. This is how we believe he spends Government time and materials.

(Military Intelligence)' and is described (in the handbook rather than the list) as 'wears glasses, is robust, fresh-faced, appears to be good natured and speaks German fluently in a mix of dialects from Saxony and Hamburg'. Hinchley-Cooke was a German specialist going back to the First World War so the Abwehr might have been expected to have identified him somehow. Number 59 in the K section of the list is 'King, M, Brit Cpt, London, White-Hal' being sought by RSHA IV E4. This is Maxwell Knight, but known to the Germans only by his cover name.

Though some of the references seem extremely fanciful (Sidney Reilly, British agent killed in Russia in 1925 is mentioned as if still alive), there are certainly allusions to genuine British agents. Though it is not clear that it is John Darwin the Gestapo seek when referring to 'Darwin, vermutl England', it seems a reasonable bet. Conrad O'Brien-ffrench appears as 'French, Marquis de Castelchomond, O'Brien, brit agent, Kapitan, vermutl England'.

So how accurate is the Black List as a list of British intelligence operatives? As we have seen, genuine British agents were identified. Conrad O'Brien-ffrench was definitely picked out, as was Norman Dewhurst, and 'Turner, dipl. Beamter, zuletz Reval/Estland' (diplomatic official, last know at Reval, Estonia) is almost certainly Stephen Turner/Sidney Tomes.

There are some apparent historical oddities. Harold Gruner, RNVR Officer and MCO from the Russian–Swedish border in 1917 (the man who strip-searched Lenin), is mentioned, though there is no evidence that he had worked for SIS or any other service since the First World War. Horribly misspelled as 'Gount, Reginald Gye, brit Admiral a D, Mitarbeiter d Intelligence Service' is Guy Gaunt, Washington naval attaché during the First World War, who had given the Germans a lot of problems, but who had abandoned intelligence work a long time before.

It is a curious collection and shows every sign of having been compiled rapidly, possibly by people who were not actually experts in the field but were given access to reports and indexes and told to do their best. Inclusion as a British agent or officer is not a guarantee that the person named actually was one, nor is their exclusion a guarantee they were not. It is probably best to consider inclusion as 'indicative' but not to be too upset if the person you are looking for is not mentioned.

Notes on reading the list

The list is only approximately in a British alphabetical order, so a thorough search of the relevant section is necessary before you can say for certain that someone you are interested in is or is not mentioned. Letter combinations of ai, ay, ei and ey are always under ai. Sch, Sp and St are listed after Sz.

The word 'Taterkreis' following several names means something like 'ring' or 'circle', though it is not obvious if this means 'spy ring' or circle of acquaintances. 'ND', which follows many, means 'secret service'. 'Deckname' is 'assumed name' or 'cover name'. 'Beamter' means 'official'.

Every entry gives the section of RSHA seeking the individual. Amt I dealt with administration and law; Amt II was responsible for investigation of the opposition; Amt III spheres of German life; Amt IV combating the opposition; Amt V criminal investigation; and Amt VI dealt with foreign intelligence. Each section had specialist sub sections – Amt IVA dealt with Communism, Marxism, the Popular Front, illegal propaganda, anti-sabotage and counter-intelligence measures, right-wing opposition, legitimism, insidious activity, ecclesiastical-political measures and emigrants. Amt IV was most interested in alleged British agents, though a few were sought by Amt VI (mainly those with a history of involvement against Russia) and Conrad O'Brien-ffrench was also sought by the Munich State Police.

There is a copy of the *Sonderfahndungsliste GB* reprinted in David Lampe's *The Last Ditch* and a facsimile edition of almost the whole RSHA handbook was published by the Imperial War Museum in 2000 under the title *Invasion 1940*, though it omits the list of suspect companies printed in Lampe's book.

Chapter 11

SPECIAL OPERATION EXECUTIVE: SECRET AGENTS AND SABOTAGE

In the late 1930s SIS began to investigate the possibility of using subversion and sabotage and established Section D to carry it out in Europe. Major Lawrence Grand was appointed to review of how this might be done. The War Office was looking at conducting guerrilla warfare in enemy occupied territory through their MI (R) department.

Grand planned to use communist organisations in Germany for general sabotage, trained individuals for special sabotage and Jews to carry out 'moral sabotage'. He began his organisation in late 1938, recruiting representatives abroad and couriers and made contact with anti-Nazi organisations. His assistant was Lieutenant Colonel Montague Chidson, a former passport-control officer (whose much redacted file is in HS 9/306/7). Early plans to sabotage shipping and to block the Danube came to nothing. Attempts to disrupt German iron-ore imports from Sweden failed when Section D's agent was arrested by Swedish police. Some useful propaganda work was done before German successes in Europe caused the collapse of almost all Section D's networks.

In August 1940 Section D produced a report detailing its achievements, most of which had been theoretical rather than practical, though they had rescued £500,000 worth of industrial diamonds from Holland and £84,000,000 worth of gold from France. They were very proud of some interesting censorship methods they had developed, but the sections detailing these have been heavily redacted.

There is a detailed (though with several redactions) file on Section D's early activities in HS 7/3 and on their activities between May and August 1940 in HS 8/214.

With most of Europe occupied Churchill decided to create an organisation for subversive warfare. Section D was subsumed within the new organisation to be called Special Operations Executive, led by labour politician Hugh Dalton, Minister for Economic Warfare. MI(R) also became part of SOE and operational control was given to Sir Frank Nelson, who took the code name CD, which passed to his successors.

SOE operated worldwide, both in occupied territory and in neutral countries. MI(R) armed Abyssinian tribesmen to fight against their Italian occupiers. SOE-trained assassins killed the brutal Reinhard Heydrich, Reichsprotektor in Czechoslovakia, unleashing ferocious reprisals on the population. In Italy, SOE's principal agent between 1941 and 1943 was

Leon Mandelstam, standing second from right, was a former Red Army soldier who served as an SOE officer in West Africa. There is no SOE personnel file for him, but he wrote about his work in From the Red Army to SOE.

actually controlled by the Italians, but it worked closely with partisans after Mussolini's fall in 1943, fighting the German occupiers. In Norway SOE-trained saboteurs destroyed the Heavy Water Plant at Rjukan, fatally delaying the German atom-bomb programme. In West Africa a former Red Army soldier, now a businessman, persuaded a Vichy French ship with a valuable cargo to leave port for capture by the Royal Navy. The film *The Sea Wolves*, in which a group of elderly Britons attack German ships in neutral Goa, was based on a real-life SOE operation. In Yugoslavia, Albania and Greece SOE missions worked with partisan groups of considerable size to fight Germans and Italians. The RAF dropped tons of supplies to these resistance groups and to the Polish Free Army fighting underground in Poland.

It was in France, Belgium and Holland where the bulk of SOE's efforts went. It was on this front that D-Day was to be launched and SOE aimed for disorganisation of German communications and disorientation and destruction of their troops. SOE agents and resistance fighters blew bridges, sabotaged trains and railways and even fought skirmishes with crack Panzer units as they moved towards Normandy. The delays they created were vital in slowing down the German build up after D-Day.

In 1945 it was suggested to Clement Attlee that SOE had established useful communications across the world that ought to continue. Attlee said that he did not want to preside over a 'British Comintern' and they should be closed down. Within forty-eight hours they were closed and, with alarming speed, its records and remaining staff taken over by SIS.

The (non) missing personnel files

SOE personnel files are in TNA's HS 9 series, comprising some 1,654 files, many of which contain details of more than 1 agent (HS 9/3 contains 11). Statistical analysis suggests there are over 13,000 individual records in the series. Legend says that only 13 per cent of personnel files survive, many having been destroyed in a fire after the war. In his book *SOE – The Special Operations Executive 1940–46*, M R D Foot states that 'SOE's total strength was never more than 10,000 men and 3,200 women', in which case almost all their files should survive. Yet there are cases that, when investigated, show absolutely that the person served with SOE but there is no HS 9 file.

There are no records for Charles Hambro, the banker who headed the Scandinavian Section and later SOE itself, for Robin Brook, Gladwyn Jebb or Lawrence Grand, all early senior SOE men, though there is one for Colin Gubbins who replaced Hambro in 1943. Polish Section's Patrick Howarth, author of *Undercover*, the excellent SOE History, does not have a file either, though this may be because he entered the 'Foreign Service' after the war – perhaps a polite way of saying SIS. Checks against some identified SOE people who only served abroad and did not come to Britain suggest that they are less likely to have HS9 files.

A random check of names from the Imperial War Museum's extensive SOE collection against the HS 9 files suggests there is a greater than 75 per cent chance that the record of any given individual is findable provided that they served within the United Kingdom at some point. Analysis of the SOE Index of Honours and Awards suggests that men and women recruited locally by SOE stations abroad are less likely to be in the HS 9 files (but it is always worth a check). The higher ranked the individual the less likely it is there will be a file. Records of many junior servicemen who were attached to SOE briefly for work in the field may not survive either. It s harder to trace women's records, partly because the fire does seem to have destroyed a section of the archive housing them. The surviving files cover operational agents (men and women who dropped into Europe) as well as training and administrative staff, including middle-ranking officers such as Maurice Buckmaster, who controlled the French Section, and general duty men at the training schools.

Unless a staff member is known to be dead, the file will be closed until 100 years have passed since their birth, though if you can prove they have died the file will be opened for you.

Some personnel files have not been released because, as TNA's website rather coyly says, 'many PFs were transferred to the personal files maintained of other government agencies for which an individual agent subsequently worked'. It would be nice to think that, if you cannot find a personnel file for someone you know was with SOE, they went on to work for SIS. Unfortunately, without other evidence you cannot really take this as proof just, possibly, as indicative.

Richard Lehniger – HS 9/907/5

A Sudeten German (Czech) who enlisted in the Pioneer Corps and changed his name to Richard Leonard, Lehniger was a 41-year-old builder and steeplejack when he came to SOE's attention in March 1941 and was codenamed 6332. He was sent to STS (Special Training School) 6, for training in Commando work, at West Court, Wokingham, which reported:

> Is highly intelligent with ample common sense that compensates for his limited education. Is looked up to as a leader by all of the others and has proved himself to be one throughout his work . . . a good disciplinarian, very keen thinking and decisive with plenty of confidence in himself . . . well connected with the Social Democratic Party and is classified B.

The Commando training centre at Arisaig House, Invernesshire, thought he had potential for leadership but 'might become too excited in a tight spot'. On 2 October 1941 he was back at STS 6 which warned:

> 6332 is a big man in more than one way, but to be useful he will have to learn that there is a time and place for everything, and that brawling won't help matters. He has far too much of a tendency to take the law into his own hands and use violence against others.

On 23 October 1941 6332 got into another fight with a member of his training group and in January 1942 it was decided to return him to the Pioneer Corps. He obviously had his supporters because STS 44, at Water Eaton Manor, Oxfordshire, reported next day:

> A pleasant tough, a born revolutionary, quite without fear of any kind. . . . he would be willing to do any dirty work, however dangerous, especially if he were well led. . . . he has taken to heart the insult of being sent back to the Pioneers. . . . In sum, he is the V.C. or Glasshouse type.

Lehniger was retained by SOE and taken onto the Operational Staff of the Commando Training School there.

Lehniger was keen to get into action and was loaned to Combined Operations for cross-channel commando raids. On 14 September 1942 SOE received notice from Combined Operations HQ that '6332 who was loaned to them by us, has been reported missing from a recent operation (Cherbourg)'. Some time later information reached the War Office from a prisoner of war that Lehniger had been killed. There is some final and sad correspondence from his widow seeking information on the circumstances of his death.

Sarah Helm's book *A Life in Secrets: Vera Atkins and the Lost Agents of SOE* contains a description of the raid in which Lehniger was killed, drawn from Imperial War Museum recordings of Lieutenant Freddie Bourne, who commanded the boat that took the party across.

> We anchored offshore about a quarter of a mile and they paddled the dory ashore. . . . Unfortunately, at that very moment when the dory was going in to land, just coming into the surf, a German patrol came along the beach. Our party was challenged and the Germans opened fire on our people just as they were getting out of their boat. The fire was returned. We got nobody back. Most of them were killed, including March-Phillipps (the commander of the raid). We had to cut the anchor to get away. A bullet went through one of our engines, so that reduced us very badly, and we turned and made our way towards the sea. One or two chaps tried to swim out, we heard them in the water, but they were too far off for us to do anything and by that time we'd got a searchlight on us and we couldn't rescue them.

A friend loaned me an excellent French book, *If I Must Die – The audacious raids of a British commando 1941 – 1943* by Gerard Fournier and Andre Heinz, which identifies the raid as 'Operation Aquatint' leading to the discovery of further files, most importantly ADM 179/227 – 'Operation Aquatint report on raid on STE. HONORINE carried out by small scale raiding party' and DEFE 2/109 containing Captain Appleyard's report. The book describes the raid in detail, including the Germans hearing a voice in the sea crying for help in fluent German when the boat was hit. Lehniger's body was recovered and he is buried at St Laurent sur Mer churchyard under his real name. Many years later his daughter visited the grave and the raid is commemorated annually in the village.

Was your ancestor with SOE?

There are records for the majority of SOE staff surviving in the HS 9 files and this is where you should begin your search. The records are alphabetical and can be viewed online at TNA's website: http://www.nationalarchives.gov.uk/catalogue, which is one of the easier search engines to use. Do not forget that a female agent or employee may be listed under her maiden name.

Service records

If you are unable trace a record in HS 9 for someone you think was in SOE and you know they were in one of the armed services, if you can, obtain their service record. Look for references to either SOE itself, or for one of its many 'cover' names such as the Inter Services Research Board (ISRB), SO2, Force 133, Force 136 or Force 139. Sometimes you might just find a note that they have been posted to a Special Training School, many of which were run by SOE.

If you can, find out which area they worked in, as the operational files are divided by geographical area so that, for example, HS 1 series cover the Far East, HS 2 cover Scandinavia and HS 3 Africa and the Middle East. Many of these files contain names of SOE officers and agents. It is worth running your eye over the HS 12 series in case your relative was recommended for an award.

SOE staff and agents

SOE staff and agents came from a wide variety of backgrounds, though intelligence and fluency in more than one language were common attribtues. Many were of dual nationality or married to a foreigner. A considerable number of soldiers and smaller numbers of sailors and airmen were posted to SOE, particularly in the Middle and Far East, Italy and

North Africa as radio operators and support administrators. A posting to SOE does not necessarily mean that a relative was involved in the more dramatic actions you might hope for.

SOE cover

SOE agents working in neutral countries used a variety of covers for their activities. In West Africa the entire Vice Consulate staff in Fernando Po were SOE men and other officers worked within the diplomatic communities in Spain, Sweden and Switzerland. Captain Hillgarth RN, the naval attaché in Madrid, commanded SOE operations in Spain in 1941. Many agents were businessmen working in areas where they were well known and had many contacts. An unusual SOE agent was Lois de Wohl, an astrologer, who did propaganda work in the USA in 1940.

SOE records – an overview

SIS took over SOE's records after the war. The reference 22666 appearing on all the HS9 files means that they were held in file 666 (someone with a sense of humour perhaps?) relating to Country 22 (Britain).

TNA website admits: 'Very few records of SOE are known to have survived . . ., following destruction . . . before the Japanese occupation of Singapore in 1942 and in Egypt before the German advance on Cairo, and subsequent weeding and a fire at SOE headquarters in 1945'. It is often possible, however, using a combination of personnel records and operational records to gain a picture of what an individual did.

The first six groups of files relate to the different areas of the world that SOE operated in and their headquarters. The general description of HS 1 applies to the other five groups of countries.

- HS 1: contains material relating to organisation, administration and activities in the Far East, including sections on Burma, Siam, French Indo-China, Malaya, China, Japan, India, Australia and the Dutch East Indies, files on black-market commodity and currency operations and currency counterfeiting. There are numerous files on personnel and training matters, war diaries and reports on operations.
- HS 2: Scandinavian Section records.
- HS 3: Africa and Middle East Section records.
- HS 4: Eastern Europe Section records.
- HS 5: Balkans Section records.

- HS 6: Western Europe Section records.
- HS 7: histories and war diaries – includes war diaries for SOE special forces and foreign missions.
- HS 8: HQ policy and planning records but names do crop up frequently. Diligent searching will be required.
- HS 9: personnel files.
- HS 10: photographs of equipment created by Station 15b used to carry out covert operations.
- HS 11: the General Nominal and Subject File Index, which has some cards referring to individuals, though it is not clear how to link the references on the card to surviving files. Worth a glance if all other attempts so far have failed to confirm a relative was with SOE.
- HS 12: a nominal card index detailing honours and awards to individuals. Cards give the subject's surname and first name, their SOE section, military rank and unit, service number, details of the award they were recommended for, name of the recommending officer, dates of recommendation, award and gazetting. Some cards have address or contact details which may help you decide if it is your relative you are looking at. These cards are often the only surviving record for SOE staff and agents recruited abroad who did not come to the UK.
- HS 13: the France Nominal Index. Important if your relative served in France or was part of the F (French) Section or RF (Free French) Section. Their index cards have been combined here with some other indexes and include such details as pseudonyms used, the SOE circuits they were involved in, details of operations participated in and accounts of their activities or roles in SOE or the local resistance, and contact addresses.
- HS 14: the Belgium Nominal Index. Contains similar details to the French Index.
- HS 15: the Italian Section and Middle Eastern and Greek Section Agent Particulars Nominal Index. These cards apparently refer only to local agents in the population whose records have not been preserved. They usually give name and address details and some information on the role they played, gathering intelligence, committing sabotage, acting as an interpreter etc.
- HS 16: Playfair and Wireless Operators Codes Nominal Card Index. Code details for each agent or wireless operator in the field, showing the letter square to be used and the phrase it was derived from, along with the security measures agents were to apply to their messages. It

is sometimes possible to identify the operator the card applied to.

• HS 17: Scandinavia Nominal Index Cards. Contains similar details to the French and Belgian Indexes.
• HS 18: Spanish and Portuguese Nominal Card Index.
• HS 19: Staff Income Tax Nominal Index Cards. Nobody knows why this small (400 card) index was created. It consists of manuscript index cards detailing for each individual (with rank where appropriate) their date of joining and leaving SOE service, PAYE status where applicable, and, for each financial year, tax due and deducted, any under or over payment, and notes that the final tax accounts had been agreed. Where the person served overseas, the dates of departure and return are noted. Some cards note if the subject joined SOE from service abroad, and, if the subject was a civilian who subsequently entered the military, the date of commission is recorded. Checks against HS 9 files suggest that only a small proportion of those in this index have personnel files (perhaps 10 per cent), so it is worth checking if no other record exists. Given the small number of cards though, it is unlikely to come up trumps if nothing has been found elsewhere.
• HS 20: the Miscellaneous Nominal Card Index.

Edith Mary Willmott – Auxiliary Units Organisation and SOE secretary

Edith Willmott was born in Bristol in 1909, a pupil of Colston's Girls' School and a graduate of the University of Bristol. Formerly secretary to an insurance manager, she joined the ATS is September 1939 and achieved rapid promotion to sergeant. A highly capable and trusted administrator, she recorded minutes of divisional and corps-level meetings at HQ Southern Command. From December 1940 she was Confidential Clerk to the Commander, Auxiliary Units, Colonel C R Major.

Applying for SOE work, she was assessed as having shorthand of 140 wpm and typing of 80 wpm, a fair knowledge of French and German and as being physically fit.

Edith, having received code and cypher training, travelled to East Africa, serving as secretary to the mission head, Lieutenant Colonel Todd. In April 1943 she was posted to Cairo for secretarial duties before being sent to Baghdad as secretary to Major Philip. From September 1943 she provided secretarial support to senior officers (including the visiting head of SOE) in Egypt and for head of G (Special Operations). In April 1945 she was in the UK but went to India, where she served until her discharge in May 1946.

SOE – other records

SOE worked in close cooperation with other government bodies so there are numerous files in their records that might prove useful.

A basic search on 'Special Operations Executive' using TNA's search engine produces 353 records held by other departments and a search under 'SOE' produces 553 records. There is a certain amount of overlap between these records but there are obviously many that might be worth exploring.

At the highest level, there are records relating to SOE in both the PREM (Prime Minister's Office) and CAB (Cabinet Office) series.

The Foreign Office files in FO 371 (Political Departments, General Correspondence) series contain a number of SOE-related files, some released only recently, presumably under Freedom of Information Act requests. These include FO 371/40001B – 'Special Operations Executive (SOE) activities in the Middle East', released in 2007, and FO 371/31321B – 'Arabia: Special Operations Executive, 1942', released in 2006. Other papers include FO 371/48496 – 'Special Operations Executive representation in Hungary' and FO 371/49963 – 'Special Operations Executive: Operations in Italy'. Do not expect too much in any of these files on individuals, particularly lower ranks and agents, but they may be useful for background information about particular areas, campaigns or policies.

The Foreign and Commonwealth Office carried out two reviews of SOE material in 1969 and 1970 and these contain some invaluable material. FCO 12/75 – 'Special Operations Executive (SOE) wartime archives' – contains discussion on surviving papers and some splendidly comprehensive bibliographies of books on SOE published up to 1969. FCO 12/166 – 'Release of war time records to Public Record Office: Special Operations Executive (SOE)' has similar bibliographies, lists of SOE members whose names were publicly known and lists of SOE members whose names were unknown at the time, along with references to War Office records that named them. It occasionally mentions SOE people whose personnel files have not survived, and there is a long list of SOE agents in France.

The majority of SOE-related papers in the FO series are in FO 954, the private office papers of Foreign Secretary Sir Anthony Eden. Dealing mainly with high-level policy matters, FO 954/24A, for example, contains a memorandum on the duties, organisation and activities of the Special Operations Executive and FO 954/24A correspondence from Hugh Dalton about the need for a high-level coordinator of propaganda and SOE activities in the Middle East.

When searching the Foreign Office indexes for SOE-related material you are likely to come across index references where the documents have not been released. Though many of these will have been destroyed, it is possible to use the Freedom of Information Act to request a check for the file and a review of any closed status.

You are more likely to find information on individuals, and on specific SOE operations, in the files of the organisations who worked most closely with them, the Army (WO series), Navy (ADM series) and Air Force (AIR series). One of the curiosities of this kind of research is that files relating to SOE, many of which name individuals and talk about operations, were released by other departments under the thirty year rule, while SOE's own files were retained.

RAF records in the AIR series very definitely require searching for using both 'SOE' and 'Special Operations Executive'. The first search term brings up 20 references but the second finds 182!

There is one pilot's log book in AIR 4 series that belonged to a pilot who flew missions for SOE. In AIR 4/96 it is for Group Captain W E Surplice DSO, DFC, who flew numerous missions over enemy territory, some of which involved work for SOE.

Records specific to SOE in the Admiralty series (ADM) on TNA's online catalogue are sparse, though for those with an interest in the history of espionage fiction there is correspondence with Commander Ian Fleming (who worked in NID) included in ADM 223/480, a file that also deals with various sabotage operations against German shipping and U-boats.

KV series (MI5 records) contain 75 references, mainly to MI5 investigations into compromised networks or suspect individuals. KV 2/2260 contains details of the LARK organisation in Norway. Members of LARK came under some suspicion but were cleared after interview. KV 2/830 is on Nicholas Bodington, regarded as a distinguished member of SOE during the Second World War, but the file is mainly concerned with unsubstantiated suggestions that he may have betrayed SOE agents to the Germans. Bodington's personal file is in HS 9/171/1.

KV 4/171 contains notes taken by an MI5 officer attending a SOE training course in February 1942. Several files in the KV 6 series relate to investigations of networks in France, Belgium and Denmark.

The Imperial War Museum collection

The Imperial War Museum (IWM) has an extensive collection of material in its documents and sound archives relating to SOE. Their online catalogue at http://www.iwmcollections.org.uk/qrymain.asp lists some 684 items using the key word 'SOE' and 795 using the keywords 'Special Operations Executive'.

IWM reference 1085/88/6/1 contains written memoirs of Wing Commander P O Hudson describing his experiences in SOE while serving with the Equipment Branch of RAF, September 1943–November 1944, his training, then service in Greece organising the building of airfields behind enemy lines to be used to receive supply drops and later as a base for the RAF. He discusses his duties, living conditions and the political situation in Greece. Hudson's as yet unopened personnel file is in HS 9/758/3 at TNA.

Other IWM collection items include nearly 200 recorded reminiscences of former SOE members, including French Resistance members, SOE officers and staff, former Section D members, wireless operators and RAF aircrew who dropped agents. The film collection includes film of sabotage devices, training films and post-war reconstructions of SOE's work. Its library holds over 200 books on SOE and related subjects.

Chapter 12

THE GOVERNMENT CODE & CYPHER SCHOOL AT BLETCHLEY PARK

Much has been written about the work of Bletchley Park and how, from small beginnings, the German machine cypher known as 'Enigma' was broken. Polish intelligence provided SIS with much information on the Enigma machine and with this assistance the systems used by the German armed forces were gradually broken. Codes and cyphers used by other countries were also cracked. Because of the extremely sensitive nature of the material it was codenamed 'Ultra' and circulated only to the very highest ranking officers and key members of their staffs. The new Director (and Head of SIS) Stewart Menzies briefed Winston Churchill personally on the key intercepts. Work on separate cyphers was done in discrete sections and staffs were forbidden to discuss their work outside their immediate colleagues. Once Ultra was publicised in 1974 several married couples discovered that they had both worked at Bletchley during the war but had never discussed it in thirty years!

There was considerable use of machines to break Enigma, most famously the 'Bombes', electromechanical devices designed by mathematician Alan Turing, and 'Colossus', the world's first digital electronic computer. Special communication units and special liaison units were established to communicate Ultra material around the world to the select group of officers allowed to receive it.

It has been estimated that the information provided by Bletchley shortened the war by two years. Certainly at times when Ultra dried up losses of shipping during the Battle of the Atlantic increased dramatically.

Tracing Bletchley Park staff

No contemporary list of Bletchley Park staff is known to have survived. There are some extant section staff lists in TNA's HW series. HW 14/9 contains a December 1940 list of all GC&CS personnel, excluding those engaged in UK cypher production at Mansfield College, Oxford. It is in alphabetical order and lists the huts staff served in, staff serving in radio-interception stations and out stations such as Wavendon, Denmark Hill and Sandridge. Sometimes, where their duties were not immediately related to code-breaking, there is a detail of their work – Mrs D I Arthur is a typist at Wavendon, Mr J C Bellinger in the Guard Room, Mr F W Buckingham an office keeper at the school, Mr T Godfrey an office keeper at Broadway (SIS Headquarters) and Private D Phillips a motor driver attached to Hut 5.

There are other staff lists throughout the HW series. HW 14/16 covers the organisation of Hut 3, which housed the analysts who interpreted the material deciphered in Hut 6 in June 1941. Commander Saunders is in overall charge, having responsibility for routing information to the Admiralty. There were six duty officers, Professor Norman, Mr Knight, Captain Douglas, Mr Marchant, Mr Barraclough and Mr Marshall, who all 'have wide experience of the whole output of five letter enigma over the last fifteen months'. Wing Commander Humphreys was in charge of the Air Intelligence officers and responsible for accurately reporting material to the Air Ministry, and Captain Curtis performed the same role for the War Office. A research section comprised Mr F L Lucas and his deputy, Miss Webb, who investigated new types of material, and Mr Saltmarsh, who linked air material with information from other sources. Major Lithgow led a party from MI 8 (a), which investigated all five-letter enigma wireless traffic. Flight Lieutenant Smith of A I 1 (e) was responsible for investigation of all RAF operational W/T intelligence from source and Mr Turner was in charge of all routing of in and out messages, typing, teleprinting and messengers. Further short lists set out the members of Wing Commander Humphreys' and Captain Curtis' teams, along with a list of all Army officers having access to Hut 3. A final list gives details of the personnel of Hut 6, which was closely linked to Hut 3, including the Army other ranks and the female ATS and civilian staff.

Searches on TNA's website for HW files with the words staff or personnel in their descriptions can be productive. HW 14/36 contains the description 'GCCS partial staff listing; staffing of AS' and it contains two short lists from 1942, one of ten WRNS who had been posted away and a list of some sixty-three technical officers and their assistants, complete with dates of birth.

HW 41/219 contains comprehensive nominal rolls and staff postings of various field-signals intelligence units from 1945, listing many hundreds of soldiers who worked either on field-interception duties or in the units that transmitted and received the Ultra decrypts.

By September 1942 there were over 2,000 staff at Bletchley and papers relating to them concentrate increasingly on shortages and ways of dealing with them. More military personnel came in, particularly WRNS, WAFF and ATS girls, whose service has not been recorded. If you can obtain their service record then there is no reason why service at GC&CS should not be released by the relevant service records office. Do not forget that postings might be shown as to SLU (Special Liaison Units), FSIU (Field Signals Intelligence Units) or GCHQ (Government Communications Headquarters).

The Bletchley Park personnel master list

A volunteer at Bletchley has compiled a two-part list of staff. Part I, drawn from contemporary wartime documents, contains some 3,800 names, along with details of the document that named them. Part II is derived from non-official sources, in particular the heritage service forms that veteran visitors are requested to complete when they visit Bletchley. There is some duplication in the lists and the possibility of error, but this list remains the most comprehensive roll of Bletchley Park staff. Bletchley Park archives are always keen to hear from former staff and their relatives and to obtain details of their service.

The Bletchley Park personnel and movement cards

Bletchley archives hold two boxes of personnel cards and movement cards, mostly dating from 1944 to 1948. There are some 3,000 cards, apparently listing correspondence relating to visitors to Bletchley, staff movements, people seeking employment, security lapses, pay and recommendations for awards. Given that there were some 8,900 staff at Bletchley at its peak in 1945 and that many of the cards deal with American visitors, other SIS officers and are from late in the war, it is clear that most staff, particularly junior ones, will not receive a mention.

For senior staff the cards can run to seven, eight or even more pages, but where junior staff are mentioned it is usually because they were posted abroad or got into trouble for lapses of security.

Wren Molly Darby's card covers arrangements for her posting for liaison work in the USA in 1945. There are queries about who is to pay for the trip and contact with WRENS HQ (HMS *Saker*) in Washington, which arranges for her travel on the *Duchess of Richmond*. In February 1946 her to return to Britain is planned for the end of March, though she is willing to continue serving until the end of May. No sooner is this agreed than she requests a return to Britain in April for personal reasons but, though this is agreed, she does not sail from New York until 1 June 1946 on the *Queen Mary*.

Cards relating to security matters go back as far as 1942 and form the earliest in the collection. Many just note a surname (not even an initial) with date and a remark such as 'talked indiscreetly' but, some contain more. Miss Doris Marjory Elrick's card reveals that she had been discovered to be a Communist with 'Risk of telling of work to Party'. Valentine Vivian (SIS Chief Security Officer) ordered that she should be 'interviewed and told of possibility of pressure by Party re details of work'. She was interviewed and allowed to remain but only a week later a letter she wrote to the Communist Party was intercepted and she was warned 'must not take active part in politics while at BP'. It seems likely that Vivian took a personal hand as a note from him states 'Has promised not to enter into enter anything controversial while in Civil Service.'

Squadron Leader John Darwin – Air Intelligence officer and spy

During the 1920s MI5 was particularly worried about technical aviation information being obtained by the Japanese or Russians and there are references in several KV files to a Flight Lieutenant (later Squadron Leader) John Darwin at the Air Ministry as their contact point. Files on Baron Sempill (KV 2/871 – KV 2/874) contain several mentions. A note says 'we intercepted a letter from Colonel Sempill to Comm. Takasu which led us to believe, after discussion with Flt Lt Darwin, that Sempill was possibly collecting certain confidential information regarding bombs for the Japanese Naval Attache'. When mail intercepts revealed that Sempill was in contact with an Air Ministry official named Fairlie, Darwin was asked to 'ascertain, if it can be done without arousing any undue attention, Fairlie's address, as he is an individual whose private life might be revelatory'.

Investigations into Alice Holland (KV 2/588) contain correspondence with Squadron Leader Darwin on communists at De Havilland aircraft works. He wrote to MI5's Major Alexander:

I have received information that the communists employed in the De Havilland Aircraft Works have started a periodical entitled 'The

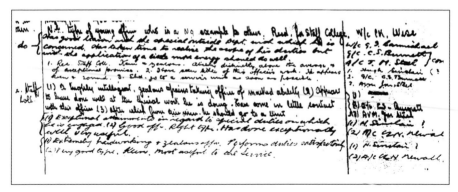

Darwin's connection with SIS is not made explicit in this extract from his service record, but the comments from, and signature of, SIS Chief Admiral Sinclair confirm his employment. (with grateful thanks to Griselda Brook)

Propellor'. . . . the only point of interest is a reference made to a secret machine being constructed at the works . . . a request for subscriptions is signed by – A Holland, 255 Goldhurst Terrace, N W 3 . . . it might be of interest to find out something more of this man, owing to the fact that experimental aircraft for the Air Ministry are being constructed at these works.

The RAF didn't have an Air Intelligence section in the 1920s and John Darwin was part of Air Operations. It is clear he had an intelligence function and was security liaison officer, but could he have had the same role with SIS? Air Intelligence files from the 1920s are particularly sparse and such searches as I made led nowhere. Some time later I was given a copy of Geoffrey Pigeon's book *The Secret Wireless War*, which contains an entire chapter on John Darwin, including the diary he wrote in 1939 and 1940 when he was working on the establishment of radio communications for SIS.

Through Bletchley Park I contacted Darwin's niece, Griselda Brook, who was researching his career. She was not aware of his MI5 connections but had already obtained a copy of his RAF service record and realised the significance of various notes on it.

Darwin's 1926 confidential report notes 'exceptional {illegible} in regard to Special Duties on which he is engaged' and is signed by H Sinclair who was, of course, Admiral Sir Hugh Sinclair.

In the 1927 Report 'C' similarly notes 'Extremely hardworking and zealous officer. Performs duties satisfactorily.'

SIS' aviation-liaison section, the existence of which has been disputed, was tucked away within the Air Ministry itself rather than at Broadway.

Darwin retired from the RAF in 1928 and went into the aviation industry, working for the Bristol Aeroplane Company and, later, Saunders Roe. He was paid a substantial retainer by Admiral Sinclair to provide information on foreign companies he was in touch with.

In 1939 Darwin returned to the RAF and to SIS, helping in the creation of their radio networks and working at Bletchley. His diary for the period is reproduced verbatim in Geoffrey Pigeon's book. Suffering from ill health, Darwin left SIS in January 1940 and returned to the RAF proper, commanding RAF Kinloss until April 1941. Ill health again dogged him and he died on Boxing Day 1941.

Chapter 13

SIS IN THE SECOND WORLD WAR

It is difficult to give a history of SIS during the Second World War from the limited records available, though hopefully the official history, due out in 2010, will redress this balance and offer pointers for further research.

In an apparent error of judgment Admiral Sinclair decided that, on declaration of the war, the 'Z' Networks were to make themselves known to the passport-control officers in their respective countries. Presumably this was to avoid the duplication of effort that had sometimes plagued the SIS and military intelligence networks during the First World War. German attempts to penetrate The Hague Office resulted in the Abwehr planting a double agent on station chief Major Richard Stephens and the 'Z' Network head in Holland, Sigismund Payne Best. Persuaded they were dealing with dissident German officers, they arranged a meeting at the Venlo crossing point and were snatched across the border. As a result of papers found on them and interrogation over many months the Germans were able to break up several SIS networks in Europe. Such was the propaganda effect of Venlo that a few SIS papers relating to the incident have been released in FO 371/23107. During the course of the Venlo debacle, Sinclair, who had been very ill, died, and was replaced by Stewart Menzies of MI1c, the War Office liaison section.

With the rapid German conquest of Western Europe SIS found itself with precious few bases from which to operate against Germany. Some kind of contact was maintained with the secret services of Vichy France (CAB 121/308) and the various countries of the Balkans became bases for action

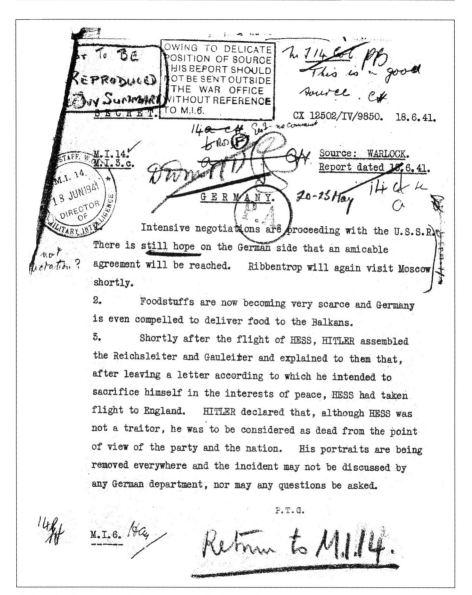

OWING TO DELICATE POSITION OF SOURCE THIS REPORT SHOULD NOT BE SENT OUTSIDE THE WAR OFFICE WITHOUT REFERENCE TO M.I.6.

CX 12502/IV/9850. 18.6.41.

Source: WARLOCK.
Report dated 16.6.41.

GERMANY.

Intensive negotiations are proceeding with the U.S.S.R. There is still hope on the German side that an amicable agreement will be reached. Ribbentrop will again visit Moscow shortly.

2.   Foodstuffs are now becoming very scarce and Germany is even compelled to deliver food to the Balkans.

3.   Shortly after the flight of HESS, HITLER assembled the Reichsleiter and Gauleiter and explained to them that, after leaving a letter according to which he intended to sacrifice himself in the interests of peace, HESS had taken flight to England.   HITLER declared that, although HESS was not a traitor, he was to be considered as dead from the point of view of the party and the nation.   His portraits are being removed everywhere and the incident may not be discussed by any German department, nor may any questions be asked.

P.T.O.

M.I.6.

SIS maintained sources inside Germany during the Second World War. This report, on reactions to Hess's flight to Britain, internal conditions and negotiations with the USSR, came from Madame Szymanska (codenamed 'Warlock'), a Polish friend of German intelligence chief Admiral Canaris, who provided SIS in Switzerland with much vital information. (with grateful thanks to Mick Smith for information on 'Warlock') against Germany, before they too fell. Switzerland and Sweden became important centres for operations. SIS was restructured so that special sections (known as 'A Sections') were created to deal with occupied countries, finding and training agents (almost always nationals of the occupied country) and sending them back via small boat, parachute or over a neutral border. It took some time to develop the kinds of networks required. Two recently released files, mostly relating to coast-watching operations in Norway and the Far East (ADM 223/884 – 'Miscellaneous SIS reports on German activity' and ADM 223/885 – 'Miscellaneous SIS reports on Japanese activity'), reveal, on analysis, that large organisations were in place by 1944 but that these were not extensive before that year.

In France the picture is different and a considerable amount of CX material was available relatively early on. Naval Intelligence files ADM 199/2462 to ADM 199/2481 evidence several SIS intelligence rings operating and supplying a constant stream of information.

SIS also enjoyed good relations with the intelligence services of other countries – the Czechs provided information from networks established before the fall of their country, and a lot of material looks to have come from the Turkish service.

If SIS gained most of its credit during the war from its ownership and circulation of Bletchley Park material it is clear that human intelligence also provided much vital information.

Tracing SIS officers and agents

Service records
Hundreds of men and women served in SIS during the war while in the armed forces and their service records can be requested from the relevant service-records offices by their next of kin. Unlike the First World War service records that were released en masse and could not therefore be weeded for SIS connections, records released individually are likely to be checked before release so redactions are going to have to be looked for. There should be no reason why SOE references are hidden, nor can I think why MI5 should be, so there is a very good chance that a redaction will mean service with SIS. Other things to look out for are SIS various cover names that might have been missed, such as Government Communications Bureau (GCB), Inter Services Liaison Department (ISLD) or even MI6. If you find anything that suggests they were 'not paid from Army Funds' this is a clue that they were being paid from the Secret Service Fund, though this could also include SOE or MI5.

Civilian staff were generally recorded as working for the Government Communications Bureau (GCB) to the extent that the Ministry of Labour complained about the similarity of the name to Government Communications Headquarters (GCHQ), which Bletchley was already using as a cover name.

SIS and other agencies

Though created out of SIS Section D, relations between SIS and SOE, at least at the top, were not always good, but there seems to have been cooperation at ground level, with interchange of staff and information. Whereas SIS was there to gather information and not disturb the Germans, SOE was there specifically to cause problems and SIS resented the large-scale manhunts the Germans launched whenever SOE succeeded. SIS ran SOE's radio communications until 1943 when SOE established its own network. SIS also insisted upon all intelligence gathered by SOE being passed to them for forwarding, though they acknowledged SOE as source.

As a result of this relationship there are files detailing cooperation at both high and local levels that might provide some clues to the diligent researcher.

HS 8/321 covers SIS/SOE relations at the highest levels, including perceived threats to SIS communications caused by SOE expansion and possible problems caused to SIS by small-scale raiding parties.

Among other files in the HS series specifically dealing with SIS that might prove useful are: HS 8/321 – 'Headquarters – SIS'; HS 1/210 – 'Andamans and Nicobars', 'SOE liaison with FO, ISLD, SIS and PWE'; HS 1/212 – 'Liaison SAS/SOE', 'Force 136', 'Clandestine ops', 'SIS reports', 'SOE reports'; HS 3/10 – 'SIS/SOE cooperation in Madagascar'; HS 3/59 – 'North Africa – Liaison arrangements: SIS, ISLD, C and MI6'; HS 4/4 – 'SIS/SOE joint effort to obtain Czech codes'; HS 6/929 – 'Co-ordination of SOE/SIS in Iberia'.

Relations with MI5 were not always cordial, particularly given SIS's Major Cowgill of Section V's obsession with security and his desire to protect SIS sources. Section V was officially accredited to MI5 as an honorary MI5 section (B26). A much-redacted file on MI5/SIS relations is in KV 2/205 and it does name some senior SIS officers.

There are numerous AIR files relating to SIS operations for dropping agents, including AIR 2/17029 – 'Bomber Command: support of SOE/SIS operations'; AIR 40/2659 – 'RAF resources made available to SIS'; AIR 20/8297 and AIR 20/8298 – '161 Squadron: reports on SIS and SOE operations'; AIR

20/8450 – 'SOE/SIS: history of Bomber Command Support'; and AIR 20/8054 – 'Mediterranean: control of aircraft operations on behalf of SOE and SIS'.

Section V

There is much material available on Section V, partly through the KV 2 files because much information MI5 received came from them, but also because Kim Philby worked in this section for a large part of the war. In his *My Silent War* he named many of his colleagues and described in detail the nature of his work. He also supplied details of the organisation to his Russian controllers and much information can be picked out of his reports to them, as published in Nigel West's *The Crown Jewels*. Many details check out against the SIS structure chart reproduced in Appendix 8. Both books should be consulted by anyone who thinks they might have an SIS relative as Philby did not hold back in naming individuals. Philby managed to obtain a key post as head of a new section, Section IX, to investigate international communism in anticipation of the threat reviving after the war. There are numerous requests in the various KV 2 files relating to Russians from the period from Section IX to MI5 and Philby's name appears to be rarely redacted.

SIS – the Bletchley Park personnel and movement cards

As Bletchley was part of the SIS organisation a few (perhaps seventy or so) personnel and movement cards give details of SIS officers where their paths crossed with GC&CS or where their promotions or movements were circulated as a matter of course.

The card for 'C' himself, Major General Sir S G Menzies KGMC, CB, DSO, MC notes that he 'Becomes Director General (reorganisation of GCCS)' on 7 March 1944 as well as various promotions and official visits and trips he made.

There are cards for other senior SIS officers including General Sir J Marshall, confirmed as joining as Assistant Chief Secret Service (ACSS) on 29 March 1943, Major General J A Sinclair (former Director of Military Intelligence), appointed Vice Chief Secret Service 3 October 1945, Captain F A Q Slocum RN, Commander P S W Sykes, Colonel V T P Vivian and Air Commodore J A Easton, appointed 'ACSS – Director of Requirements' in November 1945.

Some interesting people emerge from the cards on less-senior officers. Colonel G R Westmacott is listed as 'SIS rep in liaison with SHAEF. Whilst at Head Office he will be allotted symbol S/L = Sussex Liaison.' Colonel H H Gardiner has 'Duties as Senior Rep of CSS as Secret Intell activities against Germany att. SHAEF, working under CWE. To be known as G/L.' He is later confirmed as Head of Station in Germany on 9 August 1945 – 'Assumed Duties of 12000 in Germany'.

Lieutenant Colonel I I Milne is noted as 'Taking over from Cowgill as head of Section V' on 18 January 1945. Documents were to be addressed to him as Major Milne, MI6 V. He was awarded the OBE on 24 June 1946 and was to 'Temporarily assume duties of R8 with present duties'. Cowgill's own card notes that he is no longer head of Section V but adds that he is 'Still working at Ryder Street in Room 20, Tel ext 51'.

Sir William Stephenson, head of British Security Coordination in New York, is confirmed as SIS Head of Station by the note that he was '48000'. He was replaced as Head of Station by Colonel Wilkinson – 'Was stationed in Manila, now is 48000' (31 August 1945).

Major Bowie-MacKenzie is noted as being 'Future Chef du Bureau des Passeports a Paris', beside which someone has noted in pencil 'Passport Control?'. Bernard (no initial) is noted as 'SIS and entirely satisfactory'. Several men transferred for duties in Washington and on the move from GC&CS they also transferred into SIS. Lieutenant Cyril J B Chalkley RNVR and Captain T P Williams both 'Transferred to C's Staff' on appointment to the USA.

Lieutenant Colonel Fergusson of Section V went to India at the end of 1944 to 'deal with security matters revealed by ULTRA'. He had made some progress in setting up a Counter-E organisation when he was reported to be about to be relieved by Ionides (no card).

Lieutenant Whittaker RANVR is noted on 8 October 1945 as being the man who 'Covers MI6 interest in Dutch East Indies'. Other SIS or ISLD men in the Far East and Australasian theatres, discovered through the cards, include Major H E Martin, ISLD, 'who is also to be Security Liaison Officer in Hong Kong', Lieutenant Commander Cruickshank of ISLD noted as a 'counter-espionage agent', Commander J P Gibbs, noted as 'Controller Far East in Broadway' in March 1944, as being in Australia in May 1945 and as retiring 5 October 1945 and being replaced by Ellis with Harrison covering 'relations'.

An interesting note on the card for Commander R M Long, Director of Naval Intelligence in the Royal Australian Navy in August 1944, suggests that he might have been 'C''s Head of Station in Australia. Certainly the same hand that notes the appointment has written '? 79000 ?' on his card.

Captain G H Young has the symbol 32700/B which certainly means he is in Italy (Country 32) and, having seen the symbol on other cards, the 700 I believe to represent an officer who was cleared for Ultra.

Passport records

As with the First World War, the passport records in FO 610 series provide clues to secret-service people – in fact the clues are more than suggestive.

There is little obvious activity before September 1939, but afterwards scores of individuals travelled abroad with passports provided gratis by government ministries. Most were perfectly innocent and from the War Office, Air Ministry, Admiralty or other departments. Among the first-known SIS men are the ubiquitous Claude Dansey, granted a passport on 9 September 1939 'Gratis – On Government Service'. The same day another is granted, with the same comment, to Lancelot C De Garston , named as an SIS officer post-war in Stephen Dorrill's *MI6 – Fifty Years of Special Operations* and who also features in the Gestapo Black List. The third person granted an 'On Government Service' passport that day is Joan Constable, for whom there is yet no definite trace as SIS or other government agency.

In December 1939 we have several apparent passport-control people going about their business. William H Appleby and Norman T A Cleverley are granted gratis passports to Norway and Robert G Pinnock, Francis L Y White, Ingram A Fraser, Robert Steele, Hamish Robertson and Peter H G Newhouse to France.

In February 1940 there is an SIS Section D courier travelling 'Gratis FO', George F S Sutton, whose SOE personnel file (HS 9/1430/3) shows he began work with Section D that same month. Other known SIS men are Cuthbert Bowlby, who later headed SIS in Cairo (as the Inter Services Liaison Department), and George A Hill, formerly with SIS in Russia in 1918 and later one of SOE's representatives there.

On 7 March 1940 a 'Gratis FO' passport was issued to Roman Sudakoff, a former Imperial Russian Army officer who had served with the White Russian forces in North Russia in 1918. Sudakoff was enlisted by SIS, serving in Kovno and Vilno and, by September 1920, in Riga under the cover as a clerk in the Passport Control Office. He handled liaison with anti-Soviet émigré organisations and gathered intelligence on real or suspected Soviet agents. Sudakoff became a British subject in 1930–1931 (HO 144/14411) and continued working with Raphael Farina and Chester Giffey in the Baltic. In 1940 he was assigned to the SIS station in Turkey.

As the war progressed travel restrictions resulted in many fewer people travelling on business so the registers become increasingly full of men and women travelling on official business but the 'Gratis FO', 'PCO' and 'Government Business' passports still show up.

Among many travelling 'Gratis Passport Control' in 1943 are: Henry M Smyth, Thomas W Murrail, John M Maxey, Norman Fox, Thomas W Murray, Vera M A Aungiers, Clarice A Hammersley, Dorothy P Mingham, Gwendolen Cernat, Patricia B Retwood, Elizabeth M Leah, Richard L Dinsdale, Rupert M Beaumont, Norma B Breach, John R Cowlin, Margaret A Firebrace, Arthur L Higgs and Beryl Sutcliffe.

Some of the people travelling 'Gratis – Passport Control' are clearly SOE operatives. Leslie Hulls, sent by SOE to Russia to sabotage the Caucasus oil wells if Russia collapsed, is one, and SOE representative in West Africa Leon Manderstam is another. It may be that many of the women travelling 'Gratis – Passport Control' are SOE administrators – a comparison of people travelling under this cover from June 1943 reveals several quite definite SOE women.

A note on a Bletchley Park personnel and movement card says their passports were arranged by a Major Holditch of Flat 52, 2 Whitehall Court, an address redolent with secret-service connections going back to before the First World War. Bletchley staff going abroad travelled under a 'Gratis – Passport Control' passport.

A number of men and women can be found with 'Gratis PO Box 500' passports. These are, of course, from MI5 and some are known officers or administrators. Some do appear to have been agents.

The occasional reference is unusual and begs to be followed up. Who Herbert A Burrows, granted a passport 'Gratis Secret Business' on 30 July 1943, is or what his secret business was has yet to be revealed.

Please do not assume that just because you find a relative travelling under a gratis passport that they were necessarily up to something secretive. Try and check the Foreign Office list to see if they were employed there anyway (which does not preclude secret work) or the Imperial Calendar (available on the shelves of TNA's Open Reading Room), which lists senior civil servants with other departments. Even Passport Control, as we have seen, had a genuine function of its own, more important than ever during wartime, but still intimately connected with SIS. Try checking for their name in the Foreign Office indexes to see if you can find a file that mentions them by name, and if the file does not appear to survive then contact the Foreign Office to check and to request a copy of the Index Card if it doesn't.

ISLD – SIS cover in the Middle East and Far East

For its work in the Mediterranean and Far East SIS adopted the cover name of the Inter Services Liaison Department (ISLD).

In the Burma theatre various Special Forces such as V Force and Z Force worked behind Japanese lines to a depth of 50 or 60 miles but ISLD was responsible for deeper penetration. A sub office at Calcutta forwarded information to ISLD HQ in Delhi which passed it, in turn, to GHQ India. Head of ISLD in India for much of the war was Colonel Leo Steveni, who had served in Russia during the Intervention and as a military intelligence officer in Persia in the 1920s watching southern Russia.

Because ISLD is not as well known a cover name as MI6 there are a few more references missed by the weeders in ISLD files. A letter from Colonel Steveni to the RAF HQ in Delhi specifically requests the transfer of two Burmese aircraftsmen Saw Robert and Saw Harold Soke:

> They have been approached by a member of our Calcutta office, to whom they are personally known and to whom they have expressed their willingness to join our organisation. If we could obtain their release from the RAF and their transfer to us, they would be employed under Culley for a specific operation we are now planning.

A later letter from Steveni confirms their transfer to ISLD. The file on ISLD (AIR 23/5157 – 'Package dropping operations: Inter-Services Liaison Department No. 1') lists various ISLD operations involving RAF airdrops of agents without naming them.

WO 203/3949 – 'Inter-services Liaison Department summaries of reports' gives details of various ISLD operations in Siam, Malaya, Occupied China and Burma. Agents are not named but the reports are signed by a number of ISLD officers, including Lieutenant Colonel Van Millighem and Brigadier P Bowden-Smith as well as various illegible signatures you might recognise.

WO 204/12838 – 'ISLD operations' has been redacted but gives details of agent-dropping operations in the Central Mediterranean theatre, including drops into Italy, Czechoslovakia, Austria, Greece and Yugoslavia. Though heavily redacted, it mentions several SIS code signs and confirms, for example, that 18–land was Turkey.

HS 1/166 contains papers on ISLD relations with British Army Aid Group.

WO 208/3250 contains some information on ISLD and IS9 cooperation in the Mediterranean. WO 212/191 gives a total of 675 all ranks as the establishment figure for ISLD in January 1944.

```
                      ˙CX  REPORT


SECRET.                          CX  37442/1450   6.1.44.

M.I.2.e.                         Source:    As below.
M.I.9.

                                 Information dated: 1942 – September
                                                          1943.

                MILITARY.


     HONG KONG: Prisoner-of-war Camps

  Source:  Canadian interrogations of Miss Emily Hahn and
           Mrs. Zaitzoff repatriates in S.S. Gripsholm who left
           Hong Kong in S.S. Teia Maru September 1943.   Neither
  M.I.8b   of these sub-sources was interned.


  Common No:  1450 of 28.12.45.                     Major, G.S.

     Copies to High Commissioner Canada T Colonial Office
```

A CX report from China, 1944. Note the first line on the right-hand side of the page: the country indicator for China (37) is clearly visible, as is the fact it relates to military matters (4).

Because ISLD operated in many of the same areas as SOE and IS9 there are various files dealing with their relations. HS 5/519 – 'Relations with Inter Services Liaison Department (ISLD) and Hellenic Information Service (HIS); intrigues of Lt Cdr Noel Rees; removal of Z Boyotas from Turkey' is another heavily redacted file but names Lieutenant Commander Rees of ISLD as their man in Smyrna (Turkey), whose ambition, according to SOE, was 'to be appointed head of all Secret Service working in the Aegean. In order to achieve his goal he is jeopardising our work in the field and at times even HMG relations with the Turkish Government'.

ISLD and IS9 seem to have mounted operations together and one that went wrong is detailed in WO 208/3405 – 'MI9 staff: Noah Nussbacher' – which gives Nussbacher's description of ISLD agents codenamed 'Dickens' and 'Jones'. Jones is definitely named as 'Goldstein Feremes alias Jones, who was with Nussbacher, was sent to Germany in Dec 44 where he was engaged in March 45 in forced labour at Heinket Factory, Orienburg'.

Nussbacher also mentions ISLD agents codenamed 'Minnie and Dickens' who were travelling together. Later he mentions 'Fleishmann, Minnie's travelling companion', Fleishmann presumably being Dickens' real name.

Crawford McKay – the mysterious death of an SIS/ISLD officer

Despite disputes between SOE and SIS at high level there was a certain amount of interchange of personnel. Mostly this can just be surmised from redactions on various HS9 files but, occasionally, the weeders miss something confirming suspicions.

Lieutenant Crawford McKay's file (HS 9/1652) is thin, some eighteen pages, recording he was born on 12 August 1914 and had attended the Glasgow School of Architecture and Royal Institute of British Architecture in London. Called up in November 1940 to the Argyll & Sutherland Highlanders, he had transferred to the Royal Artillery then the Royal Engineers, where he was commissioned in January 1943. He joined SOE that year and was posted to Cairo. There is no mention of any work he did there, but seven pages of memoranda have carefully had various references redacted. They are between a redacted organisation and HQ Mediterranean concerning McKay's promotions and pay – the first, dated 23 November 1944 reads:

> It has now been approved that the above mentioned officer be promoted to the acting rank of captain wef 24 7 44 .i.e the date on which he was posted to us from his previous owners. Please take the necessary action locally.

A minute sheet dated 27 November 1944 talks about him receiving back-dated local rank rather than back-dated full promotion and has the letters CX prominent on one corner and comes from P4. P4 was the SIS production section dealing with Italy – and the minute is addressed to Naples.

Another minute sheet dated 28 June 1945 says: 'This officer was reported missing Central Mediterranean DNR Cas List 1789 (o) dated 22 Jun 1945.'

The final redacted minute is dated 19 November 1945 and reads: 'War Office Order 42/45 was published by the War Office when it was established that Capt McKay died on 11th November 1944.'

Fortunately there were some points the weeders missed, possibly because they were distracted by the obvious references they redacted. A note dated 28 September 1944 reads:

The above named officer who was posted to this organisation under your CRME/13827/AG.4(a) of 13th June 1943, has been attached to ISLD for temporary duty since June 24th 1944 and it is now desired to post him to that organisation wef date of attachment.

There is another mention of ISLD on McKay's SOE service record noting he was 'attached to No 1 IU, CMF for service in the field then Posted to No 1 IU Sec, CMF (ISLD)'. There is one clue as to where he may have served with ISLD – a very faint pencil note reads 'Jugoslavia'.

The file gives no further details, but a search of the Commonwealth War Graves Commission website (http://www.cwgc.org) reveals:

Captain CRAWFORD McKAY

259234, Royal Engineers

who died age 30 on 11 November 1944

Son of John and Jane R. R. McKay, of East Finchley, Middlesex.

Remembered with honour

KLAGENFURT WAR CEMETERY

Klagenfurt Cemetery is the only CWG Cemetery in Austria. The CWGC confirmed McKay was ISLD and that his body had been recovered from Puntingham Cemetery, Graz. This is reasonably close to the border with Yugoslavia so perhaps his operation had been in that country.

McKay's file was opened in 2004, only ninety years after his birth but there is nothing to suggest why TNA opened it or who requested it. Hopefully someone is researching him and one day his full story will be told.

Looking forward

The Official Histories MI5 and MI6 will cover the period up to the end of the Second World War. When it comes to researching into the 1950s and beyond a good starting point is to try and find what an individual did during the Second World War as there seems to have been a similar continuation of service as there was after the First World War in MI5, SIS and GC&CS (which became the Government Communications Headquarters). Service in SOE or the Intelligence Corps during the war might also be indicative of a further career in intelligence if you have other suggestions that a relative did intelligence work later on.

There is a small but steady release of intelligence-related documents to TNA. Even as this book was in its final stages ADM 223/851 – 'NID volume: Secret Intelligence Service (SIS)', which has always been closed, was opened, though with some parts redacted. It was nice to see that the information it contained supported some of my own ideas on SIS history. MI5 generally release documents every six months, usually a mixture of personal files and policy and subject files. The press usually covers the more sensational files but a lot of interesting information can be gleaned from the others. Though it would appear that all SOE's files are now at TNA there are very many personnel files that remain to be opened – a few are opened, usually after applications by researchers, every month. I have two applications in to have Home Office files relating to German agent Trebitsch Lincoln and to intercepting Russian telegrams opened, and these are still, at the time of writing, being considered.

SIS papers remain firmly closed and look likely to continue to be so for the foreseeable future. They have recently won a case brought against them by a relative of an alleged SIS German agent from the Second World War who tried to force them to confirm his role. They did have a phase of cooperating with certain researchers and allowing supervised access to their records, but I understand that this has now been withdrawn.

The task of finding secret-service ancestors is easier now than it has ever been, though it still can be a real challenge. The results however, when you get them, can be exciting and very worthwhile.

Appendix 1

OTHER ARCHIVES AND COLLECTIONS

• Churchill College Cambridge
Churchill Archives Centre
Churchill College
Cambridge
CB3 0DS
United Kingdom
Telephone: +44 (0)1223 336 087
Fax: +44 (0)1223 336 135
Email: archives@chu.cam.ac.uk

Contains extensive personal papers of people connected with intelligence – there is material on GC&CS, Air Intelligence in the Second World War and Naval Intelligence.

Details of the material can be found online at: http://www.chu.cam.ac.uk/archives/collections/classified/intelligence.php.

• Cambridge University Library
West Road
Cambridge
CB3 9DR
Tel: + 44 (0)1223 333 000
Fax: +44 (0)1223 333 160

Contains the papers of Sir Samuel Hoare, who was SIS station chief in Petrograd and Italy during the First World War, and has recently acquired papers from the family of Denis Holt-Wilson, Vernon Kell's number two at MI5 for many years.

• Imperial War Museum
Imperial War Museum London
Lambeth Road
London SE1 6HZ
United Kingdom
Email: general enquiries: mail@iwm.org.uk
Tel: general enquiries: +44 (0)2074 165 000
Fax: +44 (0)2074 165 374

As well as its important collection of SOE material already mentioned, the IWM archive holds Vernon Kell's unpublished biography, written by his wife, a recorded interview with Sigismund Payne Best describing his life as an SIS officer in both wars, interviews with a couple of SIS agents, memoirs of some MI5 Registry staff and some material on the Auxiliary Units.

Searches for material can be made online at: http://www.iwm collections.org.uk/qryMain.asp.

• Intelligence Corps Museum
Military Intelligence Museum
DISC
Chicksands
Shefford
SG17 5PR
Tel: +44 (0)1462 752 896
Fax: +44 (0)1462 752 374
Email: muscurdint-c2@disc.mod.uk

Visiting is by appointment only as the Museum is on a working military base.

• The Museum of the British Resistance
Museum of the British Resistance
Parham Airfield
Framlingham
Suffolk
IP13 9AF
Web: http://www.parhamairfieldmuseum.co.uk/brohome.html, and this links to other sites providing information on the Auxiliary Units

Appendix 2

THE MILITARY INTELLIGENCE DIRECTORATE

- MI1: the Military Intelligence Secretariat was formed in 1916 and its sub-sections dealt with distribution and registration of intelligence, investigation of enemy cyphers (MI1 (b)), secret service (MI 1(c)), intelligence summaries and security coordination.
- MI2 and MI3: these sections dealt with gathering information on and preparing reports on the armies of foreign countries. The division of responsibilities between countries varied over time but can usually be found by consulting the War Office list in TNA's Open Reading Room, which also lists the officers serving in the various directorate sections.
- MI4: the Geographical Section was responsible for the supply of all military maps and for surveying, map production and the supply of maps in the field.
- MI5: from 1916 the Security Service – in the 1920s and 1930s it appears in the War Office list as the War Office Constabulary, the cover within the War Office for the Security Service.
- MI6: in the First World War it was responsible for military policy regarding submarine cables and wireless telegraphy, cyphers, war trade and the arms trade, martial law, international law, interpreters and the internal economy of the Intelligence Directorate. In September 1939 the former SIS liaison sub-section within the War Office, MI1c, was elevated to the status of a section in its own right and renumbered as MI6 – because this was the bit of SIS that most people came into contact with the name was used generically for SIS, which is why we know it popularly as MI6 today.
- MI7: responsible for press control and the authorising of war correspondents (including photographers and film cameramen) going to the front, press censorship, study of the foreign press, examination of enemy propaganda and production of propaganda.

- MI8: in the First World War it was responsible for the censorship of telegrams and cable messages and an important part of the blockade of Germany through the commercial traffic it monitored. In the Second World War it was responsible for studying enemy radio traffic.
- MI9: in the First World War it was the section responsible for the War Office input to the postal censorship organisation. Inbound and outbound mail was checked, as was neutral mail in transit, an important source of information. By the end of 1918 it had a staff of 32 within the War Office, but over 4,500 censors were employed by the censorship department itself. There are some fascinating reports on the testing department of MI 9(c) in KV 1/73 and KV 1/74. In the Second World War MI9 was responsible for intelligence relating to British prisoners of war.
- MI10: in the First World War it was responsible for liaising with foreign military attachés and missions. During the Second World War it was responsible for technical intelligence (weapons, equipment, vehicles etc.).
- MI11: military security and field-security intelligence.
- MI12: in the Second World War postal and telegraph censorship section.
- MI14: in the Second World War it dealt with Germany, Slovakia, German-occupied Poland and the German Order of Battle.
- MI15: in the Second World War it was responsible for all matters relating to aerial photographic intelligence.
- MI19: in the Second World War it was responsible for intelligence relating to enemy prisoners of war and neutrals.
- MIR: at the end of the First World War MIR was formed to collate intelligence on Russia, Siberia, Persia, the Caucasus and areas in the Middle East considered threatened by Soviet Russia. In the late 1930s a new MIR was formed to research guerrilla-warfare techniques, leading to the establishment of the Auxiliary Units and SOE.
- MIL: in the Second World War it was the liaison section with foreign military attachés.

There is a useful history of the directorates in the First World War in WO 32/10776.

WO 106/6083 – 'History of development of Directorate of Military Intelligence 1855–1939' by Lieutenant Colonel W R V Isaac provides a detailed history of the directorates and various changes up until the start of the Second World War.

WO 208/5568 is the war diary for the directorate, along with details of the organisation and establishments.

A few war diaries for Second World War country sections of the directorate exist and provide fascinating detail on the wide-ranging sources of information they used. As well as CX material provided by SIS, they received reports from the Foreign Office, Bletchley Park, allied governments, the press and censorship.

Appendix 3

THE FIRST PASSPORT CONTROL OFFICERS

City/country	Name	Date Appointed
Greece	Mr F B Welch	23/10/19
Sweden	C H Davidson	23/10/19
	Mr R Sindall (Asst PCO)	08/04/20
	Captain J J Hitching (PCO)	
	(vice Poignant)	07/07/20
USA	Captain M Jeffes	23/10/19
	Captain J P Maine (APCO)	23/10/19
Finland	Mr G S Lennstrand (PCO)	28/10/19
	Colonel R F Meikeljohn (PCO)	10/06/20
	H A Bowe (APCO)	10/06/20
Belgium	Captain H A Westmacott	
	(vice Patterson)	29/04/20
	Mr C Webber (Asst PCO)	29/04/20
	Mr J F R Chanter (Sub PCO	
	Ostend)	18/11/19
Japan	Lieutenant Colonel D D Gunn	29/11/19
Argentina	Captain W Connon Thomson	29/11/19
Italy:		
Rome	Mr L T Williams (Asst PCO)	11/12/19
	Mr P R MacKenzie	
	(vice Gibson)	16/04/20
Milan	Mr G S Harvey (APCO)	02/09/20

Germany:

Berlin	Captain S Landau	13/01/20
	Captain E MacMichael (Asst PCO)	13/01/20
	Lieutenant Colonel N G Thwaites (vice Landau)	08/04/20
	Captain F E Foley (Asst PCO)	07/05/20
	Captain T F Brean (vice Thwaites)	01/06/20
Hamburg	Mr D S La Touche (APCO)	01/06/20
Cologne	Mr G M Lennstrand	10/06/20
	Mr J C Curtis (vice Lennstrand)	18/11/20

France:

Havre	Captain G B Johnson (Sub PCO) (vice Noble)	12/01/20
	Mr B I Southey (vice Johnson)	04/06/20
Marseilles	Lieutenant Colonel J F Corthers	08/06/20
Spain	Captain R Hollocombe (PCO) (vice Capt Cuff)	01/01/20
Bulgaria	Mr A A Elder	09/02/20
Reval	Mr L J Goodlet	16/04/20
Poland:	Captain F P Marshall (vice Bowe)	05/05/20
Warsaw	Mr W E Rodgers (acting PCO)	13/12/19
Riga	Mr H T Hall	07/05/20
Beirut	Mr E Thompson	10/06/20
Vienna	Mr A L Forbes-Dennis (PCO)	22/06/20
	Captain A J Sington (APCO)	22/06/20
Libau	Mr A W MacPherson	23/09/20
Czechoslovakia	Mr L C A Hudson (vice Capt Norman Dcsd)	19/12/20

Temporary Inspector for France, Italy and Switzerland: Lieutenant Colonel Rhys Sampson 20/08/20

Appendix 4

PASSPORT CONTROL OFFICERS

As there is no published list for these passport-control officers, the information given below is based on deductions made from other documents and so may appear inconsistent compared with Appendix 3.

Paris	Major Courtney (1940) Maurice Jeffs (1931, 1935) H T Westmacott (1927)
Belgrade	Major Lethbridge (1940)
Warsaw	Major J P Shelley (1936–1939) L Hamilton-Stokes (1934)
Brussels	E A Dalton (committed suicide 1936)
Berlin	Major Frank Foley
Finland	Ernest Boyce Harry Carr
Vienna	Mr Berry Thomas Kendrick (1938)
Prague	Captain Farrell Mr Gibson (1938)
Budapest	Captain E C Kensington (1931) Captain V C Farrell (mid-1930s) Mr P C Brown (late 1930s)

New York	Maurice Jeffs
	Maine (APCO then PCO)
	Curtis (APCO)
	Captain H B Taylor (1931)
Reval (later Tallinn)	Lieutenant Col Meikeljohn (1922)
	Chester Giffey (1938)
Riga	Mr R L J Farina
	Mr Gibson
	N Faraday (1929)
	Mr Nicholson (1934)
	K C Benton (1938)
Constantinople	A E Elder (1929)
Istanbul	Mr A Whittall (1940)

Appendix 5

SIS STATION IDENTIFIERS (OLD STYLE)

YN	New York
N	Norway
S	Sweden
D	Denmark
BN	Berlin
KL	Paris
ST	Stockholm – or Scale/Thornhill or Soviet Territory – the first specifically anti-Russian network (later Helsinki)
FB	Belgium
B	Belgium (?). Reports on Belgian munitions workers during the First World War – could be Belgian intelligence organisation as almost all reports are marked 'London'
A	?
PI	?
T	Richard Tinsley }
R	Rotterdam }
H	Holland }
FW	Rotterdam (?)
TC	" " }
TP	} Tinsley sub-agents
FR	Riga/Latvia
BP	Estonia
W	Poland (Warsaw?)
DZ	Danzig
I	Italy
G	Switzerland (?) (Geneva?)
LS	Switzerland (?) (Lausanne?)
SW	Switzerland (Berne?)

SE   Switzerland
IW   Switzerland (could be counter-Indian + W= Wallinger??)
RV   Roumania (?)
X   Spain
Z   ?
Z51   White Russian source in Berlin – Vladimir Orlov
HV   Turkey   }
Q   Turkey (?)   } An enormous amount comes out of Turkey under
RV   Turkey (?)   } all 3
MA   Greece (Athens?)
C   China
RI   Rhine Army
P   Petrograd
P   Possibly Portugal
K   Kiev (temporary in 1918)
RS   South Russia (1919/1920)
SA   South America
V   Austria (?)   Vienna (?)
MV   Austria (?)   Vienna (?)

Appendix 6

CX SOURCE IDENTIFIERS

1	FO
2	Air
3	Navy/Gas warfare
4	WO
5	Counter-Espionage
6	Industrial
7	Finance
8	Communications
9	Belgium (later 13)
10	
11	Bulgaria
12	Germany
13	Belgium
14	Roumania
15	Hungary
16	Ireland
17	Egypt
18	Turkey
19	Denmark
20	
21	Finland
22	Great Britain
23	Spain
24	Portugal
25	Albania
26	Norway
France	
27/c	Corsica
28	China
29	Czecho-Slovakia

30	
31	Latvia
Italy	
32/1	Mediterranean Italian Eastern Isles
32/S	Sicily
32/SA	Sardinia
33	Holland
34	Siberia
35	Jugoslavia
36	Sweden
Japan	
37/1	Formosa
38	Poland
39	Vatican
40	
41	Greece
42	Switzerland
43	Esthonia
44	Austria
45	
46	Lithuania
47	Ukraine
48	USA
Mediterranean, Brit	
49/1	Gibraltar
49/2	Malta
49/3	Cyprus
50	
51	Morocco and Tangier
52	Africa, It: N
53	Abyssinia
54	Africa, It: E
55	Africa Central
56	Africa N
Africa S	
58	Africa E
59	Africa W
60	
61	Afghanistan

62	India
63	Malay States
64	Tibet and Mongolia
65	Siam
66	Turkestan
67	Manchuko
68	Korea
69	Far East
70	
71	Canada
America Central/Mexico	
74	
75	America S
76	
77	
78	Philippines US
79	Australia and New Zealand
80	
81	Arabia and Transjordania
82	Iraq
83	Iran
84	
85	
86	Caucasian Republic
87	Syria
88	Palestine
89	Middle East
90	
91	Balkans
92	British possessions
93	Scandinavia
94	Third International
95	USSR
96	White Russia
97	Baltic Provinces
98	League of Nations
99	Miscellaneous

SIS STRUCTURE CHART, 1923

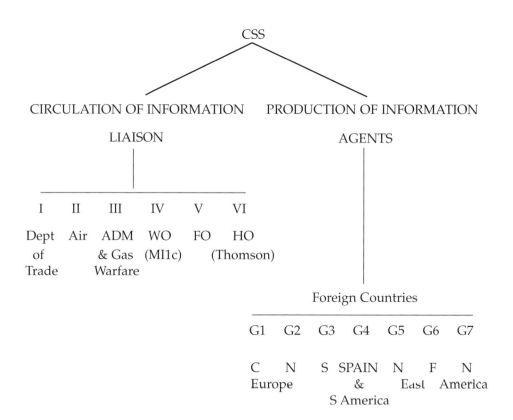

Appendix 8

SIS STRUCTURE CHART, 1943

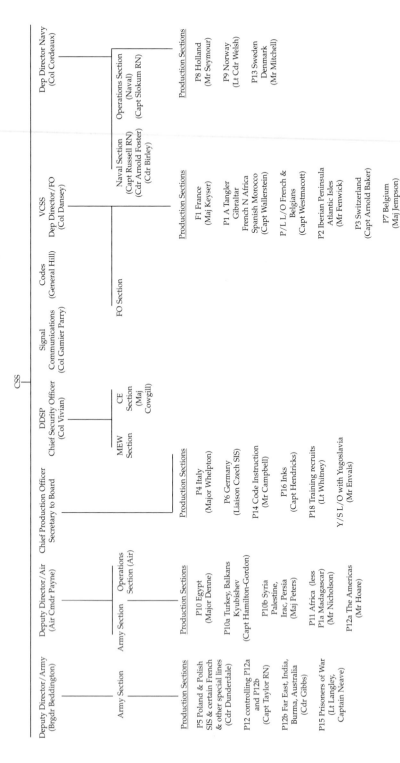

CSS

Deputy Director/Army
(Brgdr Beddington)

Army Section

Production Sections

P5 Poland & Polish
SIS & certain French
& other special lines
(Cdr Dunderdale)

P12 controlling P12a
and P12b
(Capt Taylor RN)

P12b Far East, India,
Burma, Australia
(Cdr Gibbs)

P15 Prisoners of War
(Lt Langley,
Captain Neave)

Deputy Director/Air
(Air Cmdr Payne)

Army Section   Operations
Section (Air)

Production Sections

P10 Egypt
(Major Denne)

P10a Turkey, Balkans
Kyubishev
(Capt Hamilton-Gordon)

P10b Syria
Palestine,
Irac, Persia
(Maj Peters)

P11 Africa (less
P1a Madagascar)
(Mr Nicholson)

P12a The Americas
(Mr Hoare)

Chief Production Officer
Secretary to Board

Production Sections

P4 Italy
(Major Whelpton)

P6 Germany
(Liaison Czech SIS)

P14 Code Instruction
(Mr Campbell)

P16 Inks
(Capt Hendricks)

P18 Training recruits
(Lt Whitney)

Y/S L/O with Yugoslavia
(Mr Envals)

DDSP
Chief Security Officer
(Col Vivian)

MEW
Section

CE
Section
(Maj
Cowgill)

**Signal
Communications**
(Col Gamier Parry)

Codes
(General Hill)

FO Section

VCSS
Dep Director/FO
(Col Dansey)

Naval Section
(Capt Russell RN)
(Cdr Arnold Foster)
(Cdr Birley)

Production Sections

F1 France
(Maj Keyser)

P1 A Tangler
Gibraltar
French N Africa
Spanish Morocco
(Capt Wallerstein)

P/L L/O French &
Belgians
(Capt Westmacott)

P2 Iberian Peninsula
Atlantic Isles
(Mr Fenwick)

P3 Switzerland
(Capt Arnold Baker)

P7 Belgium
(Maj Jempson)

Dep Director Navy
(Col Cordeaux)

Operations Section
(Naval)
(Capt Slokum RN)

Production Sections

P8 Holland
(Mr Seymour)

P9 Norway
(Lt Cdr Welsh)

P13 Sweden
Denmark
(Mr Mitchell)

Appendix 9

JULY 1943 PASSPORTS

Number	Name	Gratis
24525	Smith, Ruth M	Passport Control
24531	Bennitt, Marjory H W	Passport Control
24610	Nicholson, Winifred	Passport Control
24640	Tracey, Peter J	Passport Control
24765	MacFie, Helen A J	Passport Control
24766	Grant, Gillian A M	Passport Control
24767	Railton, Leonora T*	Passport Control
24774	Wigan, Thomas H#*	Passport Control
27839	Deed, Basil L	Passport Control
27840	Stephenson, Anne##*	Passport Control
24878	Tims, Barbara	Passport Control
24879	Copp, Ruth	Passport Control
24948	Roberts, Stella M*	Passport Control
24949	Wade, Muriel N*	Passport Control
24961	Duthie, Doris J D*	Passport Control
24962	Marks, Christine J N	Passport Control
24963	Wright, Ethel C C M	Passport Control
24964	Sproule, Patricia A M*	Passport Control
24965	Matheson, Heather M*	Passport Control
24966	Swithinbank, Audrey*	Passport Control
24967	Willis, Elizabeth M	Passport Control
25116	Wilson, Patricia	Passport Control
25117	Temple, Dorothy	Passport Control
25118	Tapp, Joan M*	Passport Control
25119	Dalgleish, Joan+	Passport Control
25120	Ogilvy, Margaret M+	Passport Control
25121	Newman, Marie L J*	Passport Control
25122	Bonsor, Ann E*	Passport Control
25123	Hewitt, Edna M*	Passport Control
25124	Griome, Beatrice	Passport Control

25125	Farr, Nancy E*	Passport Control
25126	Elwes, Aline M M*	Passport Control
25127	Dunn, Beryl P H*	Passport Control
25128	Dawe, Rosemary	Passport Control
25129	Hodder, Marie E*	Passport Control
25284	Lye, Florence S	Passport Control
25285	Tennyson, Harold C	Passport Control
25384	Frazer, Beryl M	Passport Control
25882	Mathews, Cynthia M	Passport Control
25604	De Salis, Charles E	Passport Control
25646	Robertson, Walter G	Passport Control
25760	Fotheringham-Parker, Rosemary###	Passport Control
25897	Caruana, Giuseppe*	Passport Control
25898	Borg, Carmelo B+	Passport Control
25929	Saunders, Malcolm G**	Passport Control
25983	Morgan, Alun M+	Passport Control
25993	Burrows, Herbert A	Secret Business
26053	Dunn, Robert	Passport Control

* Positively identified as SOE operatives.
+ Tentatively identified as SOE operatives.
** Tentatively identified as Government Code & Cypher School staff.
# Thomas Henshawe Wigan's personnel file is HS 9/1589/5. Chief agent in Brazil in 1941, he was sent to Ghana in July 1943. He fell foul of the Chief of the West Africa Mission and was sent home, saw service in the USA (no details so far found) then in the East Indies.
Anne Stephenson's personnel file is HS 9/1414/5. It confirms her as a member of the First Aid Nursing Yeomanry (FANY) and a trained radio operator who was sent to North Africa on 16 July 1943.
Rosemary Fotheringham-Parker appears in the Bletchley archive on a copy of a list of personnel in Hut 7 compiled for a re-union in London in 1947.

Bibliography

This bibliography lists all the books used in the preparation of this volume, but there are many more, of various degrees of accuracy, available. Some of the books mentioned cover more than one period.

Intelligence generally
Andrew, Chris, *Secret Service – The Making of the British Intelligence Community*, Heinemann, 1985
Smith, Michael, *The Spying Game – The Secret History of British Espionage*, Politico's, 2003

Victorian intelligence
Aston, Sir George, *Secret Service*, Faber and Faber, 1930
Baden-Powell, Lord, *The Adventures of a Spy* (originally *My Adventures as a Spy*), C Arthur Pearson Ltd, 1915
Blackburn, Douglas and Captain W Waithman Caddell, *Secret Service in South Africa*, Cassell, 1911
Robertson, Field Marshal Sir William, *From Private to Field Marshal*, Constable & Company, 1921
Waters, Brigadier General W H-H, *Secret and Confidential – The experiences of a Military Attache*, John Murray, 1926
Waters, Brigadier General W H-H, *Private and Confidential – Further experiences of a Military Attache*, John Murray, 1928

Special Branch
Brust, Harold, *I Guarded Kings – The Memoirs of a Political Police Officer*, Stanley Paul, 1938
Fitch, Herbert T, *Traitors Within*, Hurst & Blackett, 1933
Porter, Bernard, *The Origins of the Vigilant State – The London Metropolitan Police Special Branch before the WW1*, Weidenfeld & Nicolson, 1987
Porter, Bernard, *Plots and Paranoia – A history of political espionage in Britain 1790–1988*, Routledge, 1989
West, Nigel (writing as Rupert Allason), *The Branch – A History of the Metropolitan Special Branch 1883–1983*, Secker and Warburg, 1983
Woodhall, Edwin T, *Guardians of the Great*, Blandford Press, 1934

Military intelligence
Clayton, Anthony, *Forearmed – A History of the Intelligence Corps*, Brassey's, UK, 1993
Gudgin, Peter, *Military Intelligence – The British Story*, Arms and Armour, 1989
Haswell, Jock, *British Military Intelligence*, Weidenfeld & Nicolson, 1973
Morgan, Janet, *Secrets of Rue St Roch*, Allen Lane, 2004

MI5
Boghardt, Thomas, *Spies of the Kaiser – German covert operations in Great Britain during the WW1 era*, Palgrave MacMillan, 2004
Bulloch, John, *MI5 The origin and history of the British counter espionage service*, Arthur Barker Ltd, 1963

By Himself, *Commander Burt of Scotland Yard*, William Heinemann, 1959 and Pan Books, 1962

Clough, Bryan, *State Secrets – The Kent – Wolkoff Affair*, Hideaway Publications, 2005

Cook, Andrew, *M – MI5's First Spymaster*, Tempus, 2004

Curry, John, *The Security Service 1908–1945, The Official History*, The Public Record Office, 1999

Hoare, Oliver (ed.), *Camp 020 – MI5 and the Nazi Spies*, The Public Record Office, 2000

Masterman, J C, *The Double Cross System in the War of 1939 to 1945*, Yale University Press, 1972

Masters, Anthony, *The Man Who Was M – The life of Maxwell Knight, the real life spymaster who inspired Ian Fleming*, Grafton, 1986

Miller, Joan, *One Girl's War – Personal Exploits in MI5's Most Secret Station*, Brandon, County Kerry, 1986

Sillitoe, Sir Percy, *Cloak without Dagger*, Cassell, 1955

Wedderburn-Cannon, May, *Grey Ghosts and Voices*, Roundwood Press, 1976

West, Nigel, *MI5 – British Security Service Operations*, Bodley Head, 1981

Indian political intelligence
Popplewell, Richard J, *Intelligence and Imperial Defence – British Intelligence and the Defence of the Indian Empire*, Frank Cass & Co., 1995

SIS
Judd, Alan, *The Quest for C – Mansfield Cumming and the Founding of the Secret Service*, Harper Collins, 1999

Landau, Captain Henry, *Spreading the Spy Net – The Story of a British Spy Director*, Jarrolds, n.d.

Landau, Captain Henry, *Secrets of the White Lady*, Putnams, 1935

West, Nigel, *MI6*, Grafton Books, 1985

Naval intelligence
Beesly, Patrick, *Very Special Intelligence – The Story of the Admiralty's Operational Intelligence Centre 1939–1945*, Hamish Hamilton, 1977

MI9 and IS9
Foot, M R D and J M Langley, *MI9 – Escape and Evasion 1939–1945*, Book Club Associates, 1979

Langley, J M, *Fight another day – The true story of the World War II escape networks operated by MI6*, Collins, 1974

Neave, Airey, *Saturday at MI9*, Hodder & Stoughton, 1969

Bletchley Park and GC&CS
Ewing, A W, *The Man of Room 40 – The Life of Alfred Ewing*, Hutchinson & Co., 1939

Hinsley, F H and Alan Stripp (eds), *Codebreakers – The inside story of Bletchley Park*, OUP, 1993

Pigeon, Geoffrey, *The Secret Wireless War – The story of MI6 communications 1939–1945*, UPSO, 2003

Smith, Michael, *Station X: The Codebreakers of Bletchley Park*, Channel 4 Books, 2000

Smith, Michael, *The Emperor's Codes: Bletchley Park's Role in Breaking Japan's Secret Ciphers*, Bantam Books, 2001
Smith, Michael and Ralph Erskine (eds), *Action This Day*, Bantam Press, 2001
West, Nigel, *GCHQ – The Secret Wireless War*, Weidenfeld & Nicolson, 1986
Winterbotham, F W, *The Ultra Spy – An Autobiography*, Papermac, 1989

Biographies and autobiographies
Bennett, Gill, *Churchill's Man of Mystery – Desmond Morton and the World of Intelligence*, Routledge, 2007
Edmonds, H J, *Norman Dewhurst MC*, privately published by H J Edmonds, Brussels, 1968
James, Admiral Sir William, *The eyes of the Navy – a biographical study of Admiral Sir Reginald Hall*, Methuen, 1995
Mandelstam, Major L H, *From the Red Army to SOE*, William Kimber, 1985
O'Brien-ffrench, Conrad, *Delicate Mission – Autobiography of a Secret Agent*, Skilton and Shaw, 1979
Philby, Kim, *My Silent War*, Panther, 1969
Read, Anthony and David Fisher, *Colonel Z – The Secret Life of a Master of Spies*, Hodder & Stoughton, 1984
Smith, Michael, *Foley – The spy who saved 10,000 Jews*, Coronet, 1999
Whitwell, John, *British agent* (Leslie Nicholson), William Kimber, 1966

Special Operations Executive
Bailey, Roderick, *Forgotten voices of the Secret War – an inside history of Special Operations during the Second World War*, in association with the Imperial War Museum, Ebury Press, 2008
Binney, Marcus, *Secret War Heroes – Men of the Special Operations Executive*, Hodder & Stoughton, 2005
Foot, M R D, *SOE– The Special Operations Executive 1940–46*, BBC, 1984
Fournier, Gerard and Andre Heinz, *If I must Die – The audacious raids of a British commando 1941–1943*, OREP Publications, n.d., translated by Heather Costil
Howarth, Patrick, *Undercover –The Men and Women of the Special Operations Executive*, Routledge & Kegan Paul, 1980

Home Guard Auxiliary Units
Lampe, David, *The Last Ditch – The secrets of the nationwide British Resistance Organisation and the Nazi Plans for the Occupation of Britain 1940–1944*, Cassell, 1968
Schellenberg, Walter, *Invasion 1940 – The Nazi Invasion Plan for Britain by SS General Walter Schellenberg*, introduction by Professor John Erickson, St Ermin's Press, 2000
Warwicker, John (ed.), *With Britain in Mortal Danger*, Cerberus Press, 2002

Post-Second World War
Bristow, Desmond, *A game of moles – the deceptions of an MI6 Officer*, with Bill Bristow, Warner Books, 1993
Cavendish, Anthony, *Inside Intelligence – The Revelations of an MI6 Officer*, Harper Collins, 1997
Dorril, Stephen, *MI6 – Fifty Years of Special Operations*, Fourth Estate, 2000
West, Nigel, *MI5 1945–1972 A Matter of Trust*, Weidenfeld & Nicolson, 1972

INDEX